the little black book

on

Whitewater

By Brian Wilson

Edited by Timothy D. Jones

Dedications

Whenever I would think about writing a book, the required ledication" part always held a certain fascination for me. How far ck does one go in giving recognition and thanks?

God? Adam & Eve? The reproductive process? Mom and Dad? ll Gates? oops! (Sorry, I forgot I already typed in "God").

Should I "thank" Bill and Hillary Clinton & Co., without whose litical aspirations, arrogant and ignorant bunglings and lawyerly ranoias this book would not have been possible? Or, since the public would be better, healthier today had they all stayed in kansas, take 'em off the roster?

It goes without saying that friends, fans and family have been couraging and enthusiastic, much the same as a football coach uld cheer on a player who unexpectedly found himself with the ll on an open field or the way dog owners encourage a pup retriev- ; a stick. Your free copies are in the mail!

But as for the actual *dedications...*

To "President Larry" and Hughie2U, the steadfastly anonymous lividuals who got me into all this by escorting me on a guided tour Fort Marcy Park

To Tim Jones, who not only edited this, but also, for reasons own only to him, put up with late-night rations of (expletive de- ed) due largely to my ignorance of the print media and his arro- nce as a Macintosh owner.

And especially to Carol Anne Strippel who did more than time or ace or modesty allow me to mention.

Acknowledgments

Despite concerted efforts to present the information within as ntiseptically as possible (for reasons noted in the Foreword), it should e apparent to the objective reader that something is very wrong under is "umbrella" of Whitewater. So many stories of major importance ve been roundly ignored by the "mainstream media", discounted, sassembled, massaged or factually revised by the players or the spensers of what passes for news no more proof is needed to confirm e pungent, unmistakable odor of a political cover-up. Is this effort the /-product of the media's oft-stated "liberal bias"? A conspiracy of the ilaterals and the CFR? Aliens? Gas? All of the above? Who cares!!

No one with an IQ way up in double digits can dispassionately (or ccessfully) examine just the *undisputed* facts and conclude the ugly, nvoluted mess we've come to call "Whitewater" is limited to "just a led real estate deal". Or that Vince Foster wandered over to Fort arcy Park on stifling July afternoon and tried in vain to swallow a .38 ig. Or that a raft of high profile, powerful people in and out of public e did many things and did them often at least for their own personal grandizement.

A compatriot of mine, Mark Melcher, who writes the "Potomac rspective" made an interesting observation after lunch one day. He id when you tell someone you don't agree with the Warren Commis-n about Lee Harvey Oswald being the lone assassin, that he couldn't ve fired that low-rent, mail-order rifle with the speed and accuracy cessary to do his dirty work, people will stand toe-to-toe with you d refute your objections one at a time. But tell someone that Vince ster was murdered somewhere other than Fort Marcy Park, that there ere unexamined and unexplained carpet fibers all over his clothes, that ere was no dirt on his shoes after a 200 yd walk on dirt paths, that there are serious contradictions even about where the body was found and people will look you in the eye, pronounce you a bonehead, wacky a conspiracy nut —end of conversation. Of course, it has long been a tactic of the uninformed or the prejudiced to attack the messenger when the message is unacceptable. For irrefutable proof, simply review the Mike Wallace "60 Minutes" hit piece performed on Chris Ruddy.

How do these rapes of veracity continue when the singular purpose is the pursuit of the fact and truth? One explanation might be the syndrome called *"genetic fallacy"*. According to *"Modern English: A Glossary of Literature and Language"*, (Genetic fallacy) is the mistaken assumption that an idea is false or a discovery worthless because it was originated by someone we do not like.

This same fallacy, of course, may occur in Argument from Authority. Normally, the origin of an idea or discovery is irrelevant; its reliability or worth depends rather upon the weight of evidence for or against it.

It is "genetic fallacy" that has been waged against London Sunday Telegraph's Ambrose Evans-Pritchard and Pittsburgh Tribune-Review's Chris Ruddy, the two point men on the Vince Foster "suicide" story.

There are others who have made substantial contributions, and who have been likewise impugned. Some I have been able to quote like John Crudelle, New York Post and others who, for their own reasons, have steadfastly maintained their anonymity. Still others, like Hugh Sprunt and Hugh Turley have done yeomen's work winnowing facts as well as contradictions from such highly readable sources as official government transcripts, the Fiske Report, police records, etc.

There is also a cadre of talk show hosts who have been on the receiving end of collective ridicule for allegations and hypotheses we have pursued discussing Whitewater and all its subdivisions since the first story broke during the 1992 campaign. Mike Reagan, Chuck Harder, Sherman Skolnik, Zoh Hieronimus, Bob Grant and, if I may be so bold, I myself, have provided their audiences with a consistent flow

f accurate and concurrent information, as well as providing opportu-
ities to hear and speak with many of the people at the epicenter of the
ontroversy.

Then there are the folks on the Internet. Considering the abdication
f objectivity and responsibility by the "mainstream press", these people
ould constitute a new "Fourth Estate". Their intelligence and tenacity in
nding the answers has even prodded the TV and print folks along with
heir relentless pursuit, analysis and sharing of the latest information,
hanks in great measure to the technology of damn near instant global
ommunications.

To these people in particular, I offer a sincere thanks. Obviously,
his book wouldn't exist otherwise. Hopefully—and only with your
ontinued effort— the whole story may eventually see the light of day.

Someday.

For many and varied reasons, special thanks also to:

The Clinton Chronicles, Emmett Tyrell, Jr., American Spectator,
Micha Morrison, "The Mena Cover-up", Wall Street Journal, Hugh
Davies, The Daily Telegraph, Paul DeRienzo, CIA Drugs for Guns
Connection, L. J. Davis - "The Name of the Rose", The New Republic
ames Norman, Media Bypass, J. Orlin Grabbe, Larry Nichols,
Cameron Crowe, Associated Press, Reuters, CNN, Edward W. Zehr,
he Weekly Standard, Washington Times, New York Times, Washing-
on Post, Los Angeles Times, Arkansas Democrat-Gazette, Ozark
Gazette, Compton's Encyclopedia, Rick Parker, Don Williams, Jerry
eper, Jay Ring Adams, Wesley Pruden, David Brock, Michael
rbanas, Nicholas Guarino, Washington Weekly, Newsweek, Time
Magazine, US News & World Report, Walter Williams, Mark Swaney.

"Every great truth began as a heresy."

—Unknown

"Perception is Reality--but not Actuality"

— also Unknown

"Anything but the truth. It shines too hard a brilliance."

—Wesley Booth, 1971

Foreword

Greetings from an undisclosed location outside the Logic Free Zone (Washington D.C.)

While valiantly searching for a publisher for this book, I received the following in a fax from a literary agent whom I had contacted in San Francisco:

As we discussed last week, Brian...Whitewater is only tenuously clinging to the nation's attention now...On the other hand, reading the material confirmed for me that if any book on Whitewater is to be successful—and I remain skeptical of that—it's going to have to be the definitive investigative piece."

If he's right, then you are holding a book that may be the greatest literary failure since Tolstoy first just wrote "War".

But my would-be agent was right about one thing: surprisingly, few people except political wonks, rabid Clinton haters, and others with too much time on their hands can tell you much about Whitewater. It is simply too big, and seemingly too far removed from most people's immediate sphere of existence: When you're trying to juggle the rent and the phone bill, it's a little hard to keep up with which particular document was supposed to have been initialed on which day by Vince Foster. Or why Al D'Amato is so annoyingly insistent about finding out who was responsible for those mysteriously re-appearing billing records. Or even who was billing whom, and for what? Indeed, why should you care?

I have no answer to that, but if you do care, this book may provide a clue as to why so many of us are in the dark. Press coverage notwithstanding, there simply is no guide to the tremendous cast of characters, no program to help one discriminate among the arcane legalistic worms in the can called Whitewater.

And it is exactly this vacuum that this book seeks to fill — no more and no less. This is not the manifesto for a crusade, nor an investigative report. It is a guide.

Because Whitewater in all its various (and partisan) forms whips up some pretty frothy reactions in folks, Herculean efforts were made to vacuum prejudice and opinion from the contents so it would not be labeled either a Clinton "hit piece" or "cream puff". "Herculean" in that, as a radio talk show host I make my living with my opinions and try hard to influence the opinions of my audience. Conscientious talk show hosts worth their pay require themselves to be champion news junkies. As such, it was acutely obvious just how little attention the "main stream media" was devoting to the subject. As a result, by the time the stories of "Travelgate", the now-you-see-'em-now-you-see-'em-again billing records, Grand Jury Premieres and the infamous Washington Amnesia Plague finally began turning up on the evening news, many folks were behind the curve in knowing the enormous implications of what they were finally hearing, coming in on the middle of the story, so to speak. While virtually all of the information has been available in one place or another, this is the first time it has all been in one place cross-referenced and easy to read.

You will not find the answer to whether Vince Foster really committed suicide, but you will discover that serious people have alleged that he did not, who those people are, and why they disagree with the official version. There's no shocking new evidence of money laundering, gun-running, or drug transactions under Bill Clinton's nose, but I will tell you who says that was exactly the case. There are no titillating new revelations about President Clinton's alleged taste for extramarital sex, but you'll be introduced to a man who says he was hired expressly to discourage women who made such claims.

The toughest task I faced in compiling this book was knowing when to stop. The thing about Whitewater that makes conspiracy theorists drool is its utter ubiquity. Far flung events, relating to Whitewater in no immediately apparent way, seem somehow to come back to roost in Bill and Hillary Clinton's Arkansas of the '80's. Indeed, as you will read, it may not be very safe to investigate some of these enigmas at all.

However, tantalizing though these connections are, the line was drawn at the end of the several accounts expanded in the Appendices. Their inclusion here is for the purpose of providing pointers to further fascinating reading, and does not constitute an endorsement of the veracity of any such material.

I exhort interested parties to exercise compassion in their response to this work. I am not a soldier, nor are those who assisted in some way in this book. Rather, we are timid people, intellectually hobbled, slow of speech, weak of mind, of limited (and public) education, poorly equipped to deal with mercenaries, spooks or assassins.

Feel free , of course, to vent your spleen in letters or lawsuits to the appropriate parties.

Contents

1. The Players

2. Appendices

The Players

A

ADFA
Arkansas Development Finance Authority

- Arkansas state governmental organization officially established to make loans to colleges, churches, and small businesses which might have a difficult time procuring loans. By state law, the governor was required to sign all loans made by the ADFA.
- Allegedly, some of these loans were not repaid by those to whom the loans were made.

- On February 9, 1996, the federal grand jury subpoenaed ADFA to turn over copies of all files, including private correspondence, concerning POM Inc., Southern Development Bancorporation, Pine Bluff Warehouse Inc. and Can-AM Absorbents, four companies that received money from the state and AFDA.

  (*NOTE: Drug money from Mena was allegedly used to zero-out the books at the end of each month.*

  (SEE: Appendix D)

AIG
American International Group

- Multi-national insurance company allegedly involved in money laundering in Arkansas.

  (SEE: Appendix D)

AIM/AIM Report
Accuracy in Media

- Newsletter founded in 1969 by Reed Irvine "to combat political and ideological bias in the news media". Publicizes the most serious cases and mobilizes public pressure to bring about remedial action, often through full page ads purchased in the New York Times, USA Today, Washington Post, Washington Times, etc.

  (*NOTE: AIM has purchased such ads claiming errors and inaccuracies in the investigations of the death of Vince Foster. Publishes the AIM Report twice a month with copies sent to AIM members, all members of Congress, editors and reporters.*)

Ainley, Neal

Former president of the Perry County Bank (June 1989 - March 1994)

- May 25, 1990: Ainley personally delivered $30,000 from the bank to a Clinton campaign representative, then agreed with others not to file the IRS report. The first count covers his failure to file the two required IRS reports for cash transactions of more than 10,000.

- Nov. 2, 1990: The campaign withdrew another $22,500, and Ainley intercepted an IRS report prepared by another officer of the bank. The second count covers Ainley's false statement to Federal Deposit Insurance Corp. examiners that the required IRS report had been filed. In exchange for Ainley's cooperation, Ken Starr dropped five felony counts on which the federal grand jury had indicted Ainley.
  *(**NOTE**: Ainley's attorneys said he was just following orders of co-owners **Branscum** and Hill)*

- Pleaded guilty (May 1995) to reduced charges involving two misdemeanors. Sentenced in federal court (January 20, 1996) to two years probation, 416 hours of community service and a $1,000 fine for concealing large cash transactions made during Bill Clinton's 1990 gubernatorial campaign.

Altman, Roger

Former Deputy Secretary of the Treasury

- March 1993, became the acting chief of the Resolution Trust Corporation after resignation of Albert Casey.

(*NOTE: At the time, the first RTC referral involving Whitewater and Madison Guarantee had been before Paula Casey for over a year.*)

- Instructed Ellen Kulka and Jack Ryan at the RTC to block the Whitewater investigation by L. Jean Lewis.
- According to Senate Banking Committee testimony February 24, 1994, Altman arranged "heads up" meeting between president's lawyer and bank regulators.
- Later changed his story to reflect 4, then later 20, contacts between White House officials and RTC investigators. resigned his position (September 23, 1994), following congressional hearings.

   (SEE: Appendix A, Paula Casey, Jean Hanson, Web Hubbell, Jean Lewis, Whitewater, RTC)

American Spectator
Monthly news magazine

- Published several investigative articles regarding Whitewater, Troopergate, Paula Jones, Hillary Rodham Clinton, Mena, Travelgate and other scandals of the Clinton administration

Angel Fire
New Mexico resort once owned by Dan Lasater

   (SEE: Dan Lasater)

Anthony, Beryl
Vince Foster's brother-in-law.

- Worked under Webster Hubbell in the Justice Department as assistant secretary for legislative affairs. Lost his congressional seat in 1992. Joined the Washington law firm of Winston & Strawn.

Anthony, Sheila
Vince Foster's sister

- According to FBI reports, contacted an unnamed psychiatrist, explained that Foster was "working on 'Top Secret' issues at the White House and that his depression was directly related to highly sensitive and confidential matters." Foster allegedly needed assurances that nothing revealed in counseling sessions could be flushed out by subpoena at a later date.

  (SEE: Appendix C, Vince Foster)

"Arkancide"
Black humor term given to unusual number of deaths of individuals associated with Bill Clinton, Mena drug-running, etc., and the circumstances surrounding these deaths

(SEE: Appendix D, Vince Foster, Kevin Ives, Kathy Ferguson)

Arthur, Richard
Fairfax County EMS unit member

- Went to Ft. Marcy Park for Foster's body.
- Both he and Sgt. George Gonzalez questioned whether Foster's death was a suicide.

  (SEE: Appendix C)

B

Bank of Cherry Valley
Bank located in northeast Arkansas

- Owned and run by W. Maurice Smith, Jr. Smith was appointed state highway director, and later became a White House aide.
- Bank gave Clinton a $50,000 personal unsecured loan during the 1984 campaign and loaned Clinton at least $220,000 to promote his legislative agenda during the 1980s.

Barr, William P.
Former U.S. Attorney-General in the Bush Administration

Bender, John
Aviation mechanic

- In his deposition in the Reed vs. Young case, says he saw then-Governor Bill Clinton at Mena three times in the summer of 1985. No local dignitaries were present, he says, and Clinton didn't appear to be taking part in any official function. He said that Clinton arrived in a Beech aircraft, and was still there when he left for the day.

  (SEE: Mena, Buddy Young, Terry Reed, Larry Patterson, L.D. Brown)

Bennett, Robert
Washington attorney for Bill Clinton

- Argued that the President is immune from lawsuits in the Paula Jones sexual harassment suit (filed May 8, 1994). Has appealed recent (January, 1996) ruling for Jones which would allow the suit to proceed.

  (SEE: Paula Jones, "Troopergate")

Bentsen, Lloyd
Former Treasury Secretary

  (SEE: Appendix D, Robert Rubin)

Ben-Veniste, Richard
Senate Whitewater Committee's minority counsel

Berman, Mike

- President of the Duberstein Group.
- "Mondale for President" Campaign treasurer-1984.
- Was included on exclusive special access list that allowed unappointed individuals to come and go about the White House freely.

    (NOTE: The list was discontinued in 1994 after press reports questioned the practice)

- Met regularly with Foster, the first lady's chief of staff Margaret Williams, and the president.

    "Berman is raising funds for Clinton's legal defense fund, after working with White House counsel Lloyd N. Cutler in setting up the fund." (Washington Post, July 31, 1994)

Beyer, James Dr.

Deputy chief medical examiner for Northern Virginia.

- According to the Park Police report on the Foster suicide investigation, Beyer told Detective Jim Morrissette that X-rays showed no bullet fragments in Mr. Foster's head. Beyer also checked a box on the autopsy report form stating that X-rays had been taken. However, Beyer subsequently told FBI agents and Congress that no X-rays were taken because his machine was broken.

    (NOTE: According to records, the machine was installed new on June 15, 1993, and the first service call was received on October 23, three months after the suicide.)

    (SEE: Appendix C, Jesse Poor, Vince Foster)

Bianchi, Bill (Lt.)

Member, Fairfax County Fire and Rescue team.

- Called to Ft. Marcy Park. Stated James Iacaone (FCFRD) knew Foster was White House staff when he (Iacaone) returned to firehouse at 6:45 PM, in contradiction to USPP and other law enforcement testimony, according to the Fiske Report.

Billing Records

Reference to Rose Law Firm records relating to legal work performed by Hillary Rodham Clinton

- Hillary Rodham Clinton's billing records for Madison Guaranty Savings & Loan reflecting that she billed the thrift for at least 60 hours of legal services over 15 months and had many conferences with principals involved with the thrift and its developments
- Subpoenaed 1994 by federal authorities and Special Prosecutor Ken Starr
- Found (but not recognized) August 1995 by Carolyn Huber in the "book room" of the White House living quarters
- Re-discovered and significance noted by Huber January 4, 1996
- Appear to contradict public statements and sworn testimony before the Resolution Trust Corp. by Mrs. Clinton, who said she did little or no legal work for Madison
- The Clinton administration has professed mystification at their discovery.
  (**NOTE**: *Circumstances surrounding the rediscovery of the records*

resulted in the first subpoena of a First Lady, Hillary Rodham Clinton, before a Grand Jury, January 26, 1996)

(SEE: Appendix A, Castle Grande, Hillary Rodham Clinton, Web Hubbell, Rose Law Firm, Madison Guaranty S&L, Whitewater, Carolyn Huber, Seth Ward)

Blackbourne, Brian
San Diego Chief Medical Examiner

* Hired by Ken Starr to re-examine the death of Vincent Foster. Has conducted over 5,200 medical-legal autopsies, including about 1,500 involving homicides and suicides.

Black, Patricia
Associate inspector general for the Federal Deposit Insurance Corp.

* June 1995, testified before a House hearing that regulators had no evidence Hillary Clinton worked on the Castle Grande transaction
* January 1996, testified before the Senate Whitewater committee: "That answer would not have been the same had I had the billing records. We still don't know the precise nature of her involvement."

(SEE: Appendix A, Billing Records)

Blair, James
Lawyer for Tyson Foods

- Former investment advisor of Hillary Rodham Clinton who guided Mrs. Clinton through commodities trading in the late 1970's that parlayed a $1,000 investment into a $100,000 profit.
- James McDougal claims Blair was the architect of the Whitewater land deal.

  (SEE: Appendix A, McDougal, James)

Bond, Christopher
U.S. Senator R-MO

- Member of the Senate Whitewater Committee

Bone, "Red"
Investment broker for Refco

- Handled Hillary Rodham Clinton's futures trading accounts. A frequent target of professional fines, suspensions, and lawsuits.

  (SEE: Appendix A)

Boshears, Barry
Little Rock notary

- Signed Helen Dickey affidavit concerning her knowledge of death of Vince Foster

- Experts cite the affidavit's strange construction in that his signature is on a detached page and has no date, casting doubt on the validity of the document
- Boshears has refused to confirm that he issued the affidavit.

    (SEE: Appendix A, Helen Dickey, Vince Foster, US Park Police)

Branscum, Herby Jr.

Arkansas attorney and banker

Former Arkansas Democratic Chairman

Majority stock holder, Perry Country Bank of Perryville, Ark.

(SEE: Rob Hill)

Breslaw, April

Senior RTC Washington attorney

- Contradicted testimony given by Jean Lewis, a criminal investigator for the agency.

    *(**NOTE**. Ms. Lewis told the House committee that during a February 1994 meeting she had surreptitiously tape-recorded Ms. Breslaw strongly suggesting that their superiors in Washington wanted Ms. Lewis to conclude that Whitewater had not contributed to the failure of Madison Guaranty. said she did not mean to deliver such a message and Ms. Lewis had misinterpreted her remarks.)*

- Upon hearing her recorded remarks, Breslaw said since she had never heard herself on tape before, she couldn't be sure if the recording was her own voice.

    (SEE: Appendix A, Jean Lewis, RTC, Whitewater)

13

Brown, Jerry
Former Governor of California.

- First to raise issue of Hillary Clinton and Whitewater in 1992 Presidential debates.

Brown, John
Arkansas police investigator

- Assigned to investigate the Ives-Henry case
- Quoted on British TV's 20/20: "When I first reviewed the case file, I found a lot of things missing...crime scene photographs were gone, the list of evidence was gone, interviews were cut short. From 1987 until 1993 no one ever went out and talked to the people who lived by the tracks. It was never intended for this case to be solved...The concern wasn't the $400,000 in the (container of air-dropped drugs) it was the transmitter that was in the case that everyone was concerned with because it was trackable, and it would track them right back to Mena, Arkansas.... What these kids walked into was a group of law enforcement officials and drug dealers that were waiting to see who walked up onto their drop site....They were chased down, and they were taken to another location. They were beaten and held. From that they were taken and then killed. They were taken back and their bodies were placed on the tracks in hopes that all evidence of the murder would be distorted by the train mangling the bodies."
- Brown was subsequently summoned by Sheriff Judy

Pridgen, and told "John, look, you're going to have to leave this alone. We're going to...shut it down. You will interview no one who tracks this case back to Mena."

- Brown resigned the next morning.

(SEE: Appendix D, Arkancide, Kevin Ives, Fahmy Malak, Mena)

Brown, L.D.

Arkansas State Trooper

- Has repeated under oath that he was recruited by the CIA in 1984 with encouragement from then-Governor Clinton. Flew on two missions with Barry Seal to Central America to deliver M-16 rifles to the Nicaraguan Contras.

- Has sworn that on one of the trips he discovered the aircraft was carrying cocaine into Arkansas.
  (NOTE: An entry in Brown's book indicates the flight took place on October 23, 1984.)

- Confronted Clinton with this information, but says he was told not to worry.
  (NOTE: Brown alleges Clinton said "That's Lasater's deal", referring to Dan Lasater, a businessman and political supporter, later convicted on federal cocaine charges.)

- Was contacted by Ken Cargile and Dan Magruder of CIA for recruitment purposes in "paramilitary, counterintelligence and narcotics." Brown, who had worked in narcotics enforcement as a police officer, said he was interested, signed a secrecy agreement, and was told he would be contacted.

(SEE: Appendix D, Barry Seal, Mena, Dan Lasater)

Brown, Tyrone
Maintenance supervisor of Fort Marcy Park.

- Was told by "officials at the location" that Foster's body had been found by the location of the first cannon, contradicting the Fiske report, which stated the body was found near the second cannon.

  (SEE: Appendix C, Robert Fiske, Fiske Report, Vince Foster, Ft. Marcy Park)

Burton, Dan
U.S. Representative R-IN

- One of a number of Congressional critics not satisfied with the Fiske report on Whitewater and the death of Vince Foster. Personally met and questioned "CW". Discussed many of the report's discrepancies (i.e. the absence of skull bone fragments on the scene, etc.) on the House floor.

  (SEE: Appendix C, "CW", Vince Foster, Fiske Report, Ken Starr)

C

"CW"

Confidential Witness

- The "man in the white van", "CW" is the construction worker who first found Vince Foster's body.

- Claimed he inspected Foster's body "very carefully" and that Foster was not holding a gun, as the Park Police and former special counsel Robert Fiske's reports claim.

- Asked if he was certain, he said under oath (to an *ad hoc* congressional delegation headed by Rep. Dan Burton R-IN.): "As sure as I am standing here. I am absolutely and totally unequivocal, the palms were up. I looked at both palms. There was nothing in his hands."

- Claimed the FBI badgered him into saying that it was possible the gun was hidden from view by dense foliage. Also took issue with a photo leaked to ABC News that showed Foster's right thumb trapped in the trigger guard, saying "that is not a picture of what I saw."

- Has asked to remain anonymous, but has been interviewed on radio talk shows, by FBI agents, Congress and reportedly has testified before a grand jury being conducted by Special Prosecutor Ken Starr.

  (SEE: Appendix C, Ft. Marcy Park, Fiske Report, Vince Foster)

Capital Management Services
Investment company backed by the Small Business Administration

- Operated by former Judge David Hale.

    (*NOTE*: *As a "SBIC" (Small Business Investment Company), Capital was only allowed to issue loans to "disadvantaged" businesses. Capital eventually went bankrupt due to unpaid loans.*)

- Capital was involved in the following interesting transactions:

- A $300,000 loan to Susan McDougal's Master Marketing firm which was never repaid.

    (*NOTE*: *The money at one point was placed into the accounts of the Whitewater Development Corp. Allegedly under pressure from Bill Clinton to cover questionable loans for campaign debts.*)

- A $300,000 loan to Jim Tucker and his wife, allegedly for their cable television business, after Jim Tucker provided legal services for Capital Management.

    (*NOTE*: *Tucker was indicted on June 7 1995 for lying about the reason for the loan.*)

- A $65,000 loan to former Clinton aide Steve Smith's company.

    (*NOTE*: *Smith was a business partner of Jim Tucker and Jim McDougal. The loan was apparently illegally used to pay off debt on the Kings River Land Co. development, which Smith, his father, Jim Tucker, and James McDougal owned. Smith pleaded guilty to a related misdemeanor charge in a plea bargain agreement June 8, 1995.*)

- Capital borrowed $500,000 from Madison Guaranty and defaulted on the loan. (It was a real estate loan.)

    (SEE: Appendix A, Bill Clinton, David Hale, Master Marketing, Susan McDougal, Steve Smith, Jim Guy Tucker)

Cardozo, Michael
Washington investment banker

- Brought into the Justice Department in the first months of the administration. Worked/played golf with Web Hubbell. After Hubbell's resignation, gave him an office at his merchant banking firm G. William Miller & Co. Now the executive director and a trustee of the Presidential Legal Defense Trust.

Cargile, Ken
Southwest personnel representative for the CIA

- In a September 1984 letter to Ark. State trooper L.D. Brown, wrote "I am please to nominate you for employment with the Central Intelligence Agency."

    (SEE: Appendix D, L.D. Brown, Mena, Barry Seal)

Casey, Paula
U.S. attorney in Little Rock

- Appointed by President Clinton
- Refused plea bargain with David Hale who offered incriminating evidence against Bill Clinton.
- In October 1993, after one year, she formally declined to investigate any of the allegations in the first referral received from Resolution Trust Corporation.
- Later in October 1993, after the second RTC referral was reported, Casey recused herself.

    (SEE: Appendix A, David Hale)

Casey, Albert
Former RTC chief

- Replaced by Roger Altman.

    (SEE: Roger Altman)

Casolaro, Danny
Reporter investigating the Inslaw scandal

- Found with his wrists slit in the bathtub of a hotel room on August 11, 1991.

    (SEE: Appendix D, Webster Hubbel, Systematics)

Castle Grande
Real estate project of Jim McDougal

- Located on the 1,000 acres purchased from the IDC. the entire project was referred to as "Castle Grande" in the reading of the March 4, 1986, Federal Home Loan Bank examination report.
- "The land was purchased in October 1985. McDougal named the project Castle Grande [and]....dreamed of Castle Grande as an upscale working-class neighborhood featuring mobile homes, a shopping center, a convenience store and a truck stop. Castle Grande would be home to the businesses and industries that employed some of the residents."

    —*Arkansas Democrat-Gazette*
- Has been described by bank examiners as a series of "sham" transactions.

(SEE: Appendix A, Castle Grande Estates, Jim McDougal, Hillary Clinton, IDC, Seth Ward)

Castle Grande Estates

400-acre mobile-home development that was part of the 1,050-acre tract Madison and the S&L's executive Seth Ward purchased in 1985 from the Industrial Development Co. of Little Rock.

(SEE: Appendix A, Castle Grande , Jim McDougal, Hillary Clinton, IDC, Seth Ward)

Castleton, Tom

Junior White House aide

- Testifying before the Senate Whitewater Committee, said he was asked by Margaret Williams, Hillary Rodham Clinton's Chief of Staff, to carry files to the residence. These files are suspected to have been removed from Vince Foster's office the night of his death.

- Asked if Ms. Williams told him the records were needed because "President and Mrs. Clinton wanted to go through the documents" Castleton said: "My recollection is that she said the files needed to be reviewed to determine what was inside them, and that they would be reviewed by the First Lady."

  (SEE: Appendix C, Margaret Williams)

"Cattlegate"
Popular media reference to investments made by Hillary Rodham Clinton

- In 1978 and 1979, Hillary Rodham Clinton made about $100,000 in the cattle futures market. This is unusual in that even professional investors tend to lose money in this market. There is speculation that what actually happened is there were two "mirrored" accounts, which each performed opposite investments. The paperwork is suspected of having been shuffled afterwards to credit most of the profitable trades to her account and the losses to the other. According to this scenario, whoever had the other account was apparently trying to give the Clintons $100,000 under the table.

    (SEE: Appendix A, Jim Blair, Don Tyson, Tyson Foods, "Red" Bone)

Chertoff, Michael
Chief Counsel to the Senate Whitewater Committee

- 1978 graduate of Harvard Law School
- Former U.S. attorney (New York) responsible for the successful prosecution of consumer electronics tycoon "Crazy Eddie" and Genovese crime king Anthony "Fat Tony" Salerno.
- Was asked by Senator Alfonse D'Amato in spring of 1994 to be minority counsel to the Senate Whitewater Committee.

    (SEE: Appendix A)

Citizens Bank & Trust
Located in Flippin, Arkansas

- Issued the $182,500 loan for the original Whitewater property purchase.

    (SEE: Madison Guaranty Savings & Loan, Jim McDougal, Whitewater)

Clark, Ronald
Managing partner (January, 1996) at the Rose law firm.

- Acknowledged some of the billing records indicate Mrs. Clinton did 14.5 hours of work for a company involved in the Castle Grande deal and appeared to charge more than her usual rate for the work. Clark also testified that Mrs. Clinton did not tell Rose law firm partners about her personal business dealings with Whitewater partners when the firm was contemplating doing legal work for the government, which was planning to take over a savings and loan owned by the partners.

    (SEE: Appendix A, Billing Records, , Castle Grande, Hillary Rodham Clinton, Rose Law Firm, Jim McDougal, Seth Ward)

Clinger, Bill
U.S. Representative R-PA

- Chairman, House Committee on Government Reform and Oversight investigating Whitewater, Travelgate and related matters.

(SEE: Appendix A, Appendix B)

Clinton, Roger
Bill Clinton's half brother

- In 1985, was hired as a limo driver for Lasater Co. by Patsy Thomasson at Clinton's request.
- Spent 18 months in prison on cocaine possession charges, and in 1986 testified against his employer, Dan Lasater, who was also convicted on drug charges, that he "served ashtrays full of cocaine on his corporate jet", a plane used by Bill Clinton on more than one occasion.
  (NOTE: There is no material evidence that such ashtrays were present during the times Bill Clinton occupied the plane.)
- Married Molly Martin on March 26, 1994 in Dallas.

  (SEE: Dan Lasater)

Clinton, William Jefferson Blythe (Bill), IV
42nd President of the United States

- Born William Jefferson Blythe IV on August 19, 1946, in Hope, Arkansas. His father died in an car crash before his birth. Mother married Roger Clinton, and Bill took his stepfather's last name. Majored in international affairs at Georgetown University (1968.) Two years Rhodes scholar at Oxford. Graduated Yale Law School (1973), where he met Hillary

Rodham, whom he married in 1975. Returned to Arkansas as a professor at the University of Arkansas law school.

- In 1972, directed George McGovern's presidential campaign in Texas and did the same for Jimmy Carter in 1976 in Arkansas.
- In 1974, he ran for a seat in the U.S. House of Representatives.
- In 1976, he was elected attorney general of Arkansas.
- Elected governor in 1978.
- He lost a re-election bid in 1980, but won four more 2-year terms beginning in 1982.
- With regard to the Whitewater affair, Clinton is primarily alleged to have pressured David Hale, the head of an Arkansas lending agency, into making loans to Susan McDougal, the Clintons' Whitewater real estate partner.

  (SEE: Appendix A, Appendix B, Appendix C, Appendix D)

Clinton, Hillary Rodham
First Lady of the United States

- Born October 26, 1947, in Chicago.
- Majored in political science at Wellesley College, MA.
- Earned law degree at Yale, where she met Bill Clinton, whom she married in 1975, though she retained her maiden name.
- In 1976, they moved to Little Rock, Arkansas, when Bill Clinton was elected attorney general.
- Served as head of the Rural Health Advisory Committee

during Clinton's first gubernatorial term (1979-1980.)

- In 1980, became a partner in the Rose Law Firm.

- After Clinton lost his 1980 re-election campaign, she changed her image, including taking on his last name, and helped him win four more two-year terms as governor of Arkansas.

- In 1984, she was put on retainer for $2000 a month to represent Madison S&L.
  (NOTE: According to James McDougal, this was done at the governor's request due to family money problems.)

- Represented McDougal before state regulators in a possible conflict of interest.

- Performed legal services for Seth Ward, James McDougal, IDC, Castle Grande, Flowerwood Estates.

- According to recently discovered memo written by David Watkins, appears, despite her claims to the contrary, to have been the driving force behind Travelgate.

- Subpoenaed January 19, 1996, (the first First Lady ever to be subpoenaed) to appear before federal grand jury concerning the recent discovery of billing records which reflect work she did for Madison Guaranty
  (NOTE: The records had been subpoenaed for 2 years and presumed lost when they mysteriously appeared in the White House residence. They were picked up and stored by Carol Huber.)

(SEE: Appendix A, Appendix B, Appendix C, Carol Huber, Jim McDougal, Vince Foster, Travelgate, Seth Ward, David Watkins)

Coral Reinsurance

Barbados-based insurance company reportedly linked to money laundering and the ADFA

> (SEE: Appendix D, ADFA)

Cornelius, Catherine

White House aide

- Distant cousin of Bill Clinton. Lobbied to have the travel office fired and funnel its air travel functions to political and business friends.

  (SEE: Appendix B)

Crudelle, Paul

Columnist, New York Post

- Has written investigative articles about Whitewater, Mena, the death of Vince Foster and other related Clinton administration scandals.

  (SEE: Appendix A, Appendix B, Appendix C, Appendix D)

Cummings, John

Co-author, along with Terry Reed, of "Compromised: Clinton, Bush and the CIA"

> (SEE: Appendix D, Terry Reed, Iran-Contra, Barry Seal)

Cutler, Loyd

Former White House Counsel

D

D'Amato, Al
U.S. Senator R-NY

- Chairman, Senate Whitewater Committee
- Chairman, Senate Banking Committee

    (SEE: Appendix A, Appendix B, Appendix C)

Dale, Billy
Former Director of the White House Travel Office

- Testified former presidential aide Janet Green told him two days before the firings that "there is one person and only one person responsible for what has taken place with your office, and he occupies the Oval Office."
- Acquitted on charges he embezzled money from the operation.

    (SEE: Appendix B)

Davidson, James Dale
Publisher/editor, Strategic Investment Newsletter

- Commissioned a panel of 3 international experts to examine the Foster suicide note. In a triple blind test (i.e., each independent of the other) all concluded it was a forgery. Information about the lack of proper

FBI analysis of the note was highlighted in their disclosure at a press conference lightly covered by the mainstream media.

(SEE: Appendix C)

DEA
Drug Enforcement Administration

Denton, Sally
Former UPI investigative reporter

- Along with Roger Morris, former National Security Council staffer, wrote an extensive article concerning drug running and money laundering in Mena, Arkansas based on files, papers mostly from Barry Seal. Article originally scheduled to be published in Washington Post but spiked by editor at the last minute allegedly due to pressure from CIA. Subsequently published in Penthouse Magazine.

  (SEE: Appendix D)

Dickey, Helen
Former nanny to Chelsea Clinton in Little Rock and Washington

- Former social secretary in the Office of the First Lady.
- According to records, called the Arkansas governor's mansion with news of Vince Foster's death around 6 pm Central Time: "She was kind of hysterical,

crying, real upset...She told me that Vince got off work, went out to his car in the parking lot, and shot himself in the head.",according to Arkansas State Trooper Roger Perry, who took the call at the Governor's mansion.

- Issued an affidavit saying that she did not learn about Foster's death until about 10pm when she was watching TV at the White House.

  (*NOTE: Experts note, however, that the affidavit is strangely constructed. The signature of Little Rock notary, Barry Boshears, is on a detached page and has no date, casting doubt on the validity of the document. Boshears has refused to confirm that he issued the affidavit.*)

- Has since returned to Arkansas.

  (SEE: Appendix C, Roger Perry)

Dickey, Jane
Attorney, Rose Law Firm in Little Rock, AR

- Was in Washington during May 1993.
- Dined with Webster Hubbell at Washington's Galileo restaurant on May 6. Met next day with Hubbell at his office — the same day that Rose senior partner Jerry Jones arrived in Washington to confront Hubbell about his expense discrepancies that had turned up at the firm.

  (SEE: Webster Hubbell)

Dozier, Fan

Employee of Little Rock's World Wide Travel that took over part of the travel office business after the firings

- Told investigators Harry Thomason told her Mrs. Clinton would "be very upset to hear" the travel office workers had not yet been removed.

  (SEE: Appendix B, Harry Thomasson, Travelgate, David Watkins)

Duffy, Jean

Head of the Arkansas State Drug Taskforce

- Presented overwhelming evidence of the Mena drug-smuggling and its ties to the Clinton administration to members of Congress
- Has received many anonymous death threats.

Duncan, William

Former IRS agent

- Began investigating the money-laundering allegations of Barry Seal for the Internal Revenue Service in April 1983 until his transfer to Atlanta in March 1987
- Testified in July 1989 before a congressional subcommittee that he had been instructed by IRS officials to lie

to Congress about the Seal investigation.

- After the testimony, he claims the U.S. attorney's office appeared to be stalling in the case, saying both Asa Hutchinson and his successor, J. Michael Fitzhugh, dragged their feet on the investigation, failing to subpoena critical witnesses.
- Resigned from the IRS June 1989 due to IRS attorneys' pressure to perjure himself.

  (SEE: Appendix D, Duncan, Mena, Barry Seal, Russell Welch)

E

Eggleston, Neil
Former associate White House counsel

- Denied he used the power of the White House to improperly gather investigative information affecting the president as a result of what transpired at a November 5, 1993 meeting hosted by David Kendall, a private attorney for the Clintons. Bernard Nussbaum, then the White House counsel, joined Wm. Kennedy, Bruce Lindsey and Eggleston at the meeting.
  *(**NOTE:** The White House insisted the meeting was covered by attorney-client privilege.)*

- Obtained confidential files on the Small Business Administration's investigation of former Arkansas municipal judge David Hale. Said he got the files only to prepare himself to respond to press questions. Returned the files days later after learning that the Justice Department objected to their release to the White House. Did not tell FBI agents who subsequently investigated the incident that the subject of collecting records on Hale had been discussed in the Nov. 5 meeting.

- Left a telephone message for Lindsey on Nov. 16, 1993, marked "important." The subject was documents prepared by the Small Business Administration, according to a telephone log. Eggleston planned to meet an hour later with Lindsey, a former partner in the Wright Lindsey & Jennings law firm at Little

Rock, "to go over" the files.

(SEE: Appendix A, Bruce Lindsey, Bernard Nussbaum, Wm. Kennedy, David Hale, Whitewater)

Electronic Telegraph
London based news service

(SEE: Appendix A, Appendix B, Appendix C, Appendix D, Ambrose Evans-Pritchard)

"Enterprise, The"

- Alleged to be the CIA-related secret entity managed by then-Col. Oliver North and others to smuggle illegal weapons to the Nicaraguan *contra* rebels.
- According to former Drug Enforcement Agency agent Celerino Castillo and others, allegedly involved as well in a return traffic in cocaine, profits from which were then used to finance more clandestine gun-running.

(SEE: Appendix D)

Epps, Wooten
Former head of ADFA

- Replaced Bob Nash
- Named as a defendant in Larry Nichols' lawsuit.

(SEE: Appendix D, AFDA, Dan Lasater, Larry Nichols)

Espy, Mike
Former Agriculture Secretary

- Resigned under investigation by independent counsel for accepting illegal gifts from Tyson Foods.

    (SEE: Appendix A)

Evans-Pritchard, Ambrose
Investigative reporter for British Electronic-Telegraph and London Sunday Telegraph

- Reported on irregularities surrounding death of Vince Foster.

    (SEE: Appendix C)

Ewing, Hickman
Deputy Independent Counsel for Starr investigation

- Based in Starr's Little Rock office, has effectively taken over the handling of the Foster case from Mark Tuohey who resigned September, 1995

    (SEE: Appendix C)

F

Fabiani, Mark
Attorney, White House spokesman

Faircloth , Lauch
U.S. Senator R-NC

- Member, Senate Whitewater Committee

"Fat Lady from Mena"
Cargo plane, serial number 54-0679, shot down over Nicaragua in Oct. 1986

- Was carrying a load of arms destined for the Nicaraguan *contras*. Was co-piloted by a Wallace Blaine (Buzz) Sawyer who died in the crash.
  (NOTE: It was the lone surviving crew member in that downing, Eugene Hasenfus, whose admission of covert activity began a public unraveling of the Iran-contra episode.)

  (SEE: Appendix D, Mena, Barry Seal, Dan Lasater, L.D. Brown)

Ferguson, Danny
Arkansas State Trooper

- Named as co-defendant in Paula Jones' sexual harassment suit against Bill Clinton (she claims he escorted her to the governor's room.)

- Says he remembers Jones claiming that she wanted to be Clinton's girlfriend, and she gave Ferguson her phone number to give to Clinton.

  (SEE: "Troopergate")

Ferguson, Kathy

Former wife of Arkansas State Trooper Danny Ferguson

- Died from a gunshot wound to the right temple Thursday, May 12, 1994 in Little Rock. Ruled a suicide

  (SEE: "Troopergate", Bill Shelton, John Walker, Danny Ferguson, Paula Jones)

Fifth Column

Alleged rogue group of computer hackers within the intelligence community dedicated to ousting corrupt officials through blackmail

  (SEE: Appendix D)

Fiske, Robert B. Jr.

Former Special Prosecutor of the Whitewater affair

- Appointed by Attorney General Janet Reno to investigate Whitewater and the death of Vince Foster. January 20, 1994.

- Former U.S. attorney in the Southern District of New York in Manhattan from 1976 to 1980, during the Carter administration. Now a senior partner at the New York law firm of Davis, Polk and Wardwell.
- Represented key defendants in the Bank of Credit and Commerce International fraud case. Helped former law partner, independent counsel Lawrence Walsh, choose a staff to investigate the Iran-Contra scandal.

  (SEE: Appendix A, Appendix C)

Fiske Report

Product of investigation by Special Counsel Robert Fiske into the death of Vince Foster

- Concluded that the evidence was overwhelming in favor of a conclusion of suicide.
- Questioned virtually all of the major White House staff under oath, culminating with the Clintons on June 12, 1994. The Clintons were questioned separately under oath at the White House. Fiske spent 90 minutes with Bill and 60 with Hillary. They "discussed Mr. Foster's suicide and the contacts between the White House and Treasury regarding Madison Guaranty and the RTC". *Dee Dee Myers briefing, June 13, 1994.)*

Results of the Fiske investigation:

- David Hale, Eugene Fitzhugh, and Charles Matthews indicted on federal charges of defrauding the Small Business Administration of about $900,000. Hale has pleaded guilty.
- Fitzhugh and Matthews were tried and convicted (after plea bargains from felonies to misdemeanors) of

diverting funds to Hale's company, Capital Management.

- Charles Matthews: Sentenced to 18 months in federal prison
- Eugene Fitzhugh: Sentenced to 12 months in federal prison
- David Hale: Not yet sentenced

(SEE: Appendix A, Appendix C, Whitewater, Kenneth Starr, David Hale, Madison Guaranty S&L, James McDougal)

Fitzhugh, Eugene

- Indicted June 23, 1994 along with Charles Matthew and David Hale on a federal charge of conspiring to defraud the SBA.

(SEE: Appendix A)

Flowerwood Farms

Failed Arkansas land speculation deal operated by James McDougal

- Located on the outskirts of Little Rock
- Purchased April 4, 1985 by Jim McDougal with loan proceeds from Madison Guaranty S&L
  *(**NOTE**: Investigators believe Hillary Clinton co-signed this loan, which would make her personally and directly involved in McDougal's allegedly fraudulent deals. As of this writing, House and Senate committees reportedly are in possession of copies of loan papers that verify Clinton's participation)*

(SEE: Appendix A, Jim McDougal, Madison Guaranty S&L)

Fornshill, Kevin
Park Police officer

First Park Police officer to arrive at the park (after being called) and the first one who actually saw Vince Foster's body (after "CW").

(SEE: Appendix C, "CW")

Fort Marcy Park
Virginia Park where Vincent Foster's body was found on July 20, 1996

(SEE: Appendix C)

Foster, Elizabeth "Lisa" Braden
Vince Foster's wife since 1968

- The Fosters had three children together: Vincent (22), Laura (21), and John (18.)

  (SEE: Appendix C)

Foster, Shelia
Vince Foster's sister

Foster, Vincent
Deputy White House Counsel

- Handled legal matters concerning the institution of the presidency.
- Graduated Davidson College (1967.) One year Vanderbilt Law School, but left to join the National Guard. Married Lisa Braden 1968. Law degree, University of Arkansas Law School; 1971 first in his class. Former partner in the Rose Law Firm.
- Allegedly had an affair with Hillary Clinton.
- Handled the sale of the Clintons' share of Whitewater Development Corp. in December 1992.
- Died July 20, 1993. His body was found in Ft. Marcy Park, Virginia, shot in the head.
    (NOTE: Fiske Report concluded death was suicide. However, the death is still under investigation by Special Prosecutor Ken Starr)

    (SEE: Appendix A, Appendix B, Appendix C, Appendix D, Fostergate, Deborah Gorham, Web Hubbell, NSA, Rose Law Firm, Whitewater)

Friedman Paul
U.S. District Judge

- Ordered Rose Law Firm of Little Rock to release client lists going back 10 years to Resolution Trust Corporation investigators.

    (SEE: Appendix A)

G

Gale, Bob Dr.
Psychiatrist, lawyer and medical doctor

- Said James McDougal has suffered memory loss due to
  bipolar disorder and poor circulation in the brain.
  Said McDougal's lawyers could not be sure whether
  he was giving them a true recollection of events or
  versions he recalled from media coverage.

  (SEE: Appendix A, James McDougal)

Gearan, Mark
Director of the Peace Corps
Former Communications Director for President Clinton

- On February 15, 1996, the Senate Whitewater Committee
  scrutinized Gearan's notes of a Jan. 7, 1994 White
  House meeting in which Hillary Rodham Clinton
  led the White House opposition to a special
  Whitewater prosecutor; not even the president
  could get her to reconsider. Gearan's notes show
  White House aides saw themselves caught between
  Justice Department officials seeking the appointment and Mrs. Clinton opposing it. Gearan quotes
  Deputy White House Chief of Staff Harold Ickes as
  commenting that Mrs. Clinton adamantly opposed
  the appointment: "To try to reopen it (with her) ...

43

— impossible. POTUS (President of the United States) can't —staff can't,".

- According to an AP article, 2/15/96, Gearan's notes also recount then-White House Counsel Bernard Nussbaum as laying out a "scary" scenario at a Jan. 5 meeting of aides on Whitewater, in which they discussed whether the president should support appointment of a special prosecutor: "Badhearted guy goes in and decides a smell of corruption and can show some things of those people close around principal," Nussbaum is quoted as saying.

- At the Jan. 7 meeting, Gearan's notes quoted Nussbaum saying, "Indictments will be Betsey Wright."

- Gearan insisted that Nussbaum's statements were "just his very affirmative argument against an independent counsel because of its duration, its digression, that there were past instances where it went beyond, perhaps, what some people thought about it."

- As for the reference to Wright, Gearan said it was purely a hypothetical example, "an extreme example of what could really be an unwarranted prosecution."

- Gearan's notes also show Ickes referring to a career prosecutor at the Justice Department, Alan Carver, as a "bad guy." Relating a phone conversation among the Clintons' personal attorney, Carver and some FBI agents, Ickes was quoted as saying, "Those guys are (expletive deleted) us blue." Asked about the comment, Gearan testified Thursday he believed the description "bad guy" meant that Carver was tough and independent.

- Retorted committee Chairman Sen. Alfonse D'Amato, R-NY.: "A bad guy's now a tough guy?"

(SEE: Appendix A, Hillary Rodham Clinton,

Harold Ickes, Bernard Nussbaum, Betsey Wright)

Gerth, Jeff

Author of the first stories on Whitewater, published in the New York Times

> (SEE: Appendix A)

Goodwin, Tommy (Colonel)

Retired head of the Arkansas state police

> (SEE: Appendix C, Troopergate)

Gorham, Deborah

Executive assistant to Deputy White House Counsel Vince Foster

- Told Senate Committee Foster stored documents from the National Security Agency in his safe.
  > (SEE: Appendix A, Appendix C, "NSA")

Gonzalez, George (Sgt.)

- One of the first two EMS personnel to arrive at Foster's body in Ft.. Marcy Park. Along with Richard Arthur, Gonzalez questions Foster's death as a suicide.
- In contradiction to the Fiske report, he has consistently maintained Foster's body was found near the first

Civil War cannon and not the second which is deep inside the park

(SEE: Appendix C)

Grabbe, Orlin

Prolific writer of Whitewater related articles

*(**NOTE**: Name believed to be a pseudonym)*

H

Hale, David (Judge)
Appointed as a municipal judge by Governor Clinton

- Convicted of defrauding the Small Business Administration for loaning $300,000 to Susan McDougal which was never repaid. Ran Capital Management Services, Inc., which was legally required to loan money only to the "disadvantaged."

- Stated that the loan was to "clean up" problems involving "the political family." On the same day that Vince Foster "committed suicide", Hale's Little Rock office was raided by federal investigators.

- Indicted September 1993 on federal charges of defrauding the Small Business Administration of $800,000. (*NOTE: This indictment was later replaced by a similar one issued by Fiske*)

- General Accounting Office report (21 March 1994) documented several shell companies he set up to illegally distribute more than $3.4 million in Small Business Administration funds. —*March 22, 1994,* **USA Today**

- Has provided important information to the Fiske and Starr investigations. Agreed to a plea bargain for his role, pleading guilty to two federal crimes: deliberately overstating the amount of capital in his investment company to qualify it for SBA. loan funds, and

loaning money to individuals not qualified under SBA guidelines.
- Allegedly in the Witness Protection Program.

    (SEE: Appendix A, Fiske Report)

Haley, John
Little Rock attorney

- Personal lawyer to Govenor Jim Guy Tucker
- Indicted June 7, 1995 on felony count of helping Tucker and William Marks hide assets to reduce tax liability
- Pleaded not guilty

Hamilton, James
Washington attorney

- Graduated from Davidson College (same as Vince Foster).
- Yale Law graduate.
- Assistant Chief Counsel, Senate Select Committee on Presidential Campaign Activities (Watergate Committee) 1973-74 (with Bernard Nussbaum and Hillary Clinton.)
- Author of: *The Power of Probe: A Study of Congressional Investigations*, Random House 1976.
- Articles include: "Congressional Investigations: Legal Issues and Practical Approaches", "Kurland, Watergate and the Constitution", "Nixon's Weak Hold Over Haig Tapes", "Executive Privilege: A New Face-Off", "The Carter Briefing Scandal", "Can Congress Make Lawyers talk?", "Sleaze Factor Can

Be Avoided", "A Legislative Proposal for Resolving Executive Privilege Disputes Precipitated By Congressional Subpoenas", "Iran - Contra Ruling Immunities Limits", Attorney-Client Privilege in Congress," and many more.

- Was part of Clinton's transition team as Clinton - Gore transition Counsel for Nomination and Confirmation 1992-1993
- Helped select Supreme Court Justice Ruth Ginsberg.
- Was featured on "60 Minutes" as Foster family lawyer.
- Made numerous requests to Attorney General Janet Reno to have Vince Foster "suicide note" returned to Foster family
- Required to be present for all FBI interviews of Lisa Foster, all of which were held in Hamilton's office
- According to the Martindale-Hubbell Law Directory, Mr. Hamilton's Practice areas are: Government Affairs Litigation and Criminal Law.

    (SEE: Appendix C)

Hanson, Jean
Former Treasury Counsel

- Provided former Deputy Secretary of the Treasury Roger Altman with "heads-up" concerning possible criminal referrals from RTC concerning Bill and Hillary Clinton's involvement with Jim McDougal and Madison Guaranty S&L.
- Testified that Harold Ickes had asked her not to tell anyone about her conversation with Roger Altman about his decision to recuse himself from Whitewater matters in the RTC.

(NOTE: Ickes said during the hearings that he had no recollection of making those statements. Hanson and Altman both resigned after the hearings)

- Resigned August 18, 1994

  (SEE: Appendix A, Roger Altman, Jean Lewis, Harold Ickes, RTC, Whitewater)

Haut, Donald (Dr.)

Fairfax County Medical Examiner

- Arrived at Ft. Marcy Park to examine Vince Foster's body. He actually rolled the body over. Claims Foster's body was 10 to 20 yards past an old civil war cannon, which is direct contradiction to the Fiske Report, but corroborates Sgt. George Gonzalez' statement.
- Told the FBI that upon his arrival, everyone present at the scene knew Foster was with the White House, in contradiction to the Fiske Report.

  (SEE: Appendix C, Sgt. George Gonzalez, Fostergate, Ft. Marcy Park, Fiske Report)

Hawkins, Sarah

Compliance officer for Madison Guaranty Savings and Loan Association

- Defense attorneys said Hawkins was prepared to testify that documents showing that Madison Guaranty had complied with lending laws were lost some time after government regulators took over the institution. Hawkins' attorney advised her to assert her right against self-incrimination after learning that she would not be granted immunity from prosecution.

(SEE: Appendix A, Madison Guaranty)

Henrickson, Joseph
Tyson Foods employee

- Told Donald Smaltz that six times he carried envelopes with a quarter-inch thick stack of $100 bills to Little Rock, where the money was allegedly transferred to then-Governor Bill Clinton.

  (NOTE: Mr. Smaltz told Time magazine that "based upon the way this story unfolded, it has the ring of truth to it," noting that Mr. Henrickson did not volunteer the account until after a day of tough questioning.)

  (SEE: Appendix D, Mike Espy, Donald Smaltz, Tyson Foods)

Hedges, Jeremy
One of two college students employed as couriers in the Rose Law Firm

- Hedges says in late January 1994, after the special counsel began his Whitewater investigation, he and another courier, Clayton Lindsey, spent an hour shredding materials marked VFW from the office of Vince Foster, who had handled some of the Clintons' Whitewater dealings, and who had committed suicide in July 1993
- At a meeting with managing partner Ronald Clark and others a few weeks later, they were informed that

they would have to answer FBI questions and testify before the Whitewater grand jury.

- Says when they were told to tell the FBI he had shredded Foster documents, Rose attorney Jerry Jones replied, "Don't assume they were his documents." According to Hedges, when he answered in turn that he was certain, Jones told him, "Don't assume that they have anything to do with the investigation."

    (SEE: Appendix A, Rose Law Firm, Vince Foster, Whitewater)

Henry, Don

Teenage boy found dead along with Kevin Ives near Mena, Arkansas

> **(SEE: Appendix D)**

Heuer, Sam

Attorney for Jim and Susan McDougal

Hill, Rob

Co-Owner, Perry County Bank

- Employed Neal Ainley

    (SEE: Ainley, Neal)

Howard, George Jr (Judge)

U.S. District Judge

- Judge hearing the trial of Arkansas Govenor Jim Guy Tucker and co-defendants James and Susan McDougal

Huber, Carolyn
Director, White House Personal Communication

- Former office manager, Rose Law Firm
- Told the Senate Whitewater Committee (January 19, 1996) that in early August 1995, she unexpectedly discovered Hillary Rodham Clinton's missing billing records in the book room of the White House residence. Said they were folded but in plain view, on a pile of books on the corner of a table where they hadn't been just days earlier.

  (*NOTE: The billings had been subpoenaed for 2 years and presumed lost or shredded. While the residence area of the White House is restricted to the First Family, guests and servants, neither Bill or Hillary Clinton professed any idea how the records came to be there. The originals are still missing.*)

  (SEE: Appendix A, Billing Records, Roger Altman, Jean Lewis, Harold Ickes, RTC, Whitewater)

Hubbell, Suzanna
Wife of Webster Hubbell

- In attempting to get a position with the government, Mrs. Hubbell contacted associate White House counsel Bruce Lindsey. The stated purpose of the call was to see if he could check on the status of the approval. The job has completely different duties from her previous position, but is at the same pay level. It is believed that the Hubbell family is financially troubled, partially based on his 1993 confirmation hearings which revealed $570,000 in debts ($400,000 of that is a mortgage). Ken Starr is now investigating to see if the job was related to the agreement.

Hubbell, Webster

Former Mayor of Little Rock

Former managing partner Rose Law Firm

Former Associate Attorney General (third-ranking official in the Justice Department)

- Drafted the legislation, Act 1062, which created the ADFA.

  (*NOTE: Rose Law Firm, was in charge of investigating all applicants for ADFA loans; Seth Ward, Hubbell's father-in-law, was first one to benefit from an ADFA loan, an apparent conflict of interest.*);

- Had custody of the billing records that detailed Hillary Rodham Clinton's hours worked in representing Madison Guaranty S&L as well as Hubbell's father-in-law, Arkansas tycoon Seth Ward, on the real estate deal called Castle Grande.

  (*NOTE: The records were gathered up during the 1992 presidential campaign and kept at times in Hubbell's basement.*)

- December 1994, pleaded guilty to defrauding clients, tax evasion and mail fraud in connection with overbilling of the Federal Deposit Insurance Corporation and the Resolution Trust Corporation.

- Sentenced to 21-months in prison, 3 years probation, and $135,000 in restitution in plea bargain with Ken Starr, sentenced to 21 months.

  (*NOTE: Hubbell's sentencing was postponed twice to allow Starr more time to question him and evaluate the extent of his cooperation.*

He was questioned about Vince Foster as a part of the grand jury investigation. There are allegations that the White House tried to influence his testimony through his wife, Suzanna Hubbell, rehired February 6,1995 at the Interior Department shortly after the plea bargain agreement was announced, following an eleven month leave of absence from the politically appointed $60,925/year position.)

(SEE: Billing Records, Castle Grande, Suzanna Hubbell, IDC, James McDougal, PoM, Rose Law Firm, Seth Ward)

I

Ickes, Harold
Deputy White House Chief of Staff

- Testified before House and Senate Banking Committee hearings investigating improper contacts between White House and Justice Department regarding RTC referrals from Jean Lewis naming Bill and Hillary Clinton in possible involvement in illegal check schemes.

- Quoted in notes dated January 7, 1994 as saying "Bev Bassett is so f——— ipt (important). If we f— this up, we're done. Let's not talk it to death. Let's get it done. We can't send PB, BL MW—it will come out. Item by item—make sure her story is OK." This was a reference to the upcoming testimony of Beverly Basset Schaffer, former head of the Arkansas State Securities Department

    (NOTE: Presidential Special Counsel Jane Sherburne identified MW as Michael Waldman, a staff member of the White House communications department. There was no identification of PB and BL but Pat Begala was a Clinton political consultant and Bruce Lindsey is a Clinton friend and advisor.)

    (SEE: Appendix A, RTC Beverly Basset Scaffer)

IDC Project
Industrial Development Co.

- Held the mortgage on 1,050 acres of the partially developed Little Rock Industrial Park in southern Pulaski County, Arkansas (Castle Grande)

- In October 1985, IDC sold this land to interest controlled by James McDougal for $1.75 million. Regulations prevented Madison Financial, the real estate subsidiary of Madison Guaranty S&L, from investing more that $600,000, and Seth Ward held the balance of $1.15 million, financed by a non-recourse loan from Madison.

  *(**NOTE**: Madison loan officer Don Denton has said former deputy attorney general Webster Hubbell, Mr. Ward's son-in-law, had drafted Mr. Ward's 1985 promissory note with Madison for the purchase of the Castle Grande project.)*

- Federal investigators have characterized Mr. Ward's role as a "straw" purchaser and found most of the sales "had been to insiders acting as straw buyers."

- The Resolution Trust Corp. is investigating the $400,000 option deal Mr. Ward made with McDougal and Madison Guaranty S&L.

  *(**NOTE**: According to Rose Law Firm, a code on the option document indicates it was authored by Hillary Rodham Clinton. Rose billing records for Hillary Clinton show a number of conversations with Seth Ward while these deals were being consummated. Former Madison president John Latham testified in court that the purpose of the option was to provide a way for Mr. Ward to get about $356,000 in commissions on the Castle Grande project that Mr. McDougal agreed to pay him in a side deal without the approval of the Madison Guaranty board. When questioned by the RTC in 1995, Clinton claimed she didn't know, didn't recognize and hadn't worked on "Castle Grande," said she only "worked on IDC".)*

- The location of the sales trailer where, according to David Hale, then-Governor Clinton and McDougal pressured him to lend Susan McDougal $300,000 — a charge both Clinton and McDougal deny.

  (SEE: Appendix A, Castle Grande, Hillary Clinton, David Hale, Web Hubbell, James McDougal, RTC,

Seth Ward, Whitewater)

Inslaw
Inslaw, Inc.

Small software company owned by William and Nancy Hamilton

- Wrote software, called PROMIS, for tracking bank funds.
- In 1982, signed a $10 million contract with the Justice Department to install their PROMIS software into offices of forty-two U.S. Attorneys. Incurring heavy debt, Inslaw obtained a loan to complete the contract, but upon installation the Justice Department refused to pay, thus forcing them into bankruptcy.
- Inslaw accused the Justice Department and the National Security Agency of stealing the software and using it to track international money laundering.
- The week before the death of Vince Foster's death, Inslaw forwarded a rebuttal to an internal Justice Department report on the alleged software theft to Webster Hubbell, then Assistant Attorney General. Inslaw later learned that Web Hubbell owned stock in Systematics, the Arkansas firm that distributed the software and was also a lawyer for the firm.

  (SEE: Appendix D, Vince Foster, Web Hubbell, Jim Norman, Jackson Stephens,)

Isikoff, Michael
Former reporter for the Washington Post

- Reportedly suspended for insubordination after his

editors "spiked" an article he had been preparing on
Paula Jones, and on other women who alleged
similar experiences with Bill Clinton.
*(NOTE: Reportedly, as a result of this incident, Isikoff left the Post
to join Newsweek magazine)*

Ives, Kevin

**Ives and another teenage boy, Don Henry, were
found dead August 23, 1987 on railroad tracks near
the Intermountain Airport in Mena, Arkansas**

**(SEE: Appendix D, Fahmy Malak, Mena, Don
Henry)**

J

Jennings, Alston
Little Rock, Ark., lawyer representing Seth Ward

- Called before the Senate Whitewater Committee due to an August 1995 meeting at the White House with Hillary Clinton that corresponded with the mysterious re-appearance of missing subpoenaed billing records.
- Testified before the Senate Whitewater Committee (2/96) he and Mrs. Clinton discussed legal work they had done as adversaries in the past, to help prepare the first lady for an anticipated attack "concerning her ability as a lawyer."

  (SEE: Appendix A, Billing Records, Hillary Rodham Clinton, Park-O-Meter, Seth Ward)

Johnson, Jim (Judge)
Former Arkansas Supreme Court Justice

- Has given a series of broadcast and print interviews highly critical of Bill Clinton's activites as Govenor and as President.

Jones, Jerry
Attorney, Rose Law Firm, Little Rock, Ark.

- Had begun calling Web Hubbell in Washington on February 3, 1992, a few weeks after Bill Clinton's inauguration.
- Met with Hubbell May 7 re: expense/billing discrepancies less than two weeks before Hubbell's Senate confirmation Hearing on May 19.
- Kept leaving messages for Hubbell, (42 total), until he stopped calling in February 1994 - shortly before Rose leaked word of the discrepancies to the press. Hubbell resigned from the Justice Department in March 1994, and was indicted nine months later.

  (SEE: Web Hubbell, Rose Law Firm)

Jones, Paula
Plaintiff in $750,000 sexual harassment suit against Bill Clinton

- The suit was filed May 8, 1994. the result of an incident that allegedly occurred on May 8, 1991
- Substance: Jones was working at the registration desk at a trade fair at the Excelsior Hotel in Little Rock as a junior employee of the Arkansas Industrial Development Commission when a state trooper (Danny Ferguson) informed her that the governor wished to speak to her. She assumed that this was concerning job prospects and went up to his room. In a sworn affidavit, she states, "The Governor made a series of unwelcome sexual advances, each of which were unmistakably rebuffed." She stated that Clinton pulled his trousers down and asked her to perform oral sex. She described his behavior as boorish and grotesque. When she tried to get away, she alleges,

Mr. Clinton let it be known that her boss was a personal friend of his. "I was really afraid of losing my job," she said.

—*The London Sunday Telegraph*

• The White House denies the story and says that Mr. Clinton never met her. However, two of her colleagues have signed affidavits corroborating significant parts of her story. While neither was a witness of the alleged encounter, both say that she related the details immediately afterwards and was shocked and humiliated. On May 8, 1994, her lawyer, Daniel Traylor, filed a complaint (after several delays), the last day possible before the statute of limitations would have expired. The lawsuit accuses Clinton of "conspiracy to deprive plaintiff of her federally protected rights under the 5th and 14th Amendments to the U.S. constitution and for intentional infliction of emotional distress," and "willful, outrageous and malicious conduct." Jones says any proceeds from the suit would be donated to a Little Rock charity.

(**NOTE**: *Clinton claimed to have not returned to the hotel that afternoon, but the featured speaker at the conference has stated that he saw Clinton there at that time.*)

K

Kendall, David
Private attorney for the Clintons

- Hosted November 5, 1993 meeting with Bernard
  Nussbaum Wm. Kennedy III, Bruce Lindsey and
  Neal Eggleston in the offices of Williams &
  Connolly. Discussed, among other things, collecting
  records on David Hale.
  *(NOTE: This was the meeting at which Wm. Kennedy took his now
  infamous notes, subsequently turned over to the Senate Whitewater
  Committee but not until after the Senate voted to enforce the
  subpoena in court. The White House insisted the meeting was
  covered by attorney-client privilege.)*
- Subpoenaed to appear before the Grand Jury (January,
  1996) in the matter of Hillary Clinton's mysteriously
  re-appearing Rose billing records. During his testimony, Kendall questioned the credulity of Carolyn
  Huber, who discovered the records.

  **(SEE: Carolyn Huber, Bernard Nussbaum, Wm.
  Kennedy, Bruce Lindsey, Neal Eggleston, David
  Hale, Senate Whitewater Committee)**

Kennedy, William III
Former Associate White House Counsel
Current Rose Law firm partner

- In charge of background investigations into White House
  personnel. Allegedly allowed hundreds of people

who should have been denied clearance to hold positions with access to classified documents.

- Called in the FBI to provide cover for the firings of the Travel Office employees intimating the case was of interest "at the highest levels".
- On July 20, 1993, accompanied by his Special Assistant Graig Livinstone, went to morgue to identify Vince Foster the night of his alleged suicide.
- Author of the now-infamous notes of a November 1993 Whitewater strategy session meeting in the office of Williams & Connolly with the Clinton's private attorney, David E. Kendall.
- Told the Senate Whitewater committee that the reference to "vacuum Rose law files" in his handwritten notes referred to the "vacuum of information" regarding the files — their state of disorder.
- Now believes he misread his own handwriting and he actually wrote the word "Quality," not "Quietly," referring to the poor quality of the files.
- Dismissed as Associate White House Counsel after it was revealed he failed to pay Social Security taxes for household help.
- Reassigned to "other duties" on March 23, 1994.
- "At his request, Associate Counsel William Kennedy, who has been responsible for vetting the background of presidential appointees and for supervising the issuance of White House passes, has been transferred to other duties within the Counsel's office. His former responsibilities will be assumed by the Associate Counsel Beth Nolan."

—*White House press release statement by then-Chief of Staff and White House Counsel Lloyd Cutler*

- Has recently returned to Rose law firm

(SEE: Appendix A, Travelgate)

Kingston Bank & Trust
Bank located in Kingston in northwestern Arkansas

- Was owned by James McDougal, Susan McDougal, and Stephen Smith.
  (*NOTE: Kingston was later renamed to Madison Bank & Trust and should not be confused with Madison S&L.*)
- Loaned Hillary Clinton $30,000 in December 1980, which she used to build a model house on a Whitewater lot, given to her for free by the Whitewater Development Corporation. Whitewater Development later assumed responsibility for the loan.
  (*NOTE: Reportedly, these transactions were not properly reported on tax returns.*)

Knowlton, Pat
First person to find Vince Foster's car at Fort Marcy Park, July 20, 1993 approximately 4:30pm

(*NOTE: Foster's body was found more than an hour later.*)

- Knowlton told the FBI he saw a man who [stood] next to Foster's car giving him a menacing look. Knowlton quickly left the park.
- Reported incident to US Park Police.
- Reported incident to Robert Fiske's FBI investigators.
  (*NOTE: In an interview with Ambrose Evans-Pritchard who showed him a copy of his FBI statement, he said the FBI falsified his statement, claiming he could not identify the man that was sitting in the car whereas he said he most certainly can identify the man.*)
- Supplied information for a police artist sketch.

- Appears to have been monitored around his Pennsylvania Avenue residence in Georgetown under a massive surveillance operation.
- Has testified before Ken Starr's Washington, DC grand jury.

   (SEE: Appendix C)

L

Lasater, Dan
Little Rock business man and personal "FOB"

- Was one of the largest contributors to Clinton's many campaigns.
- First met Clinton in the late seventies when Lasater got a racetrack box for Clinton's mother, Virginia Kelley.
- In the early '80's, started a bonding company, Lasater & Company, and hired Patsy Thomasson as the company's Vice President, at Clinton's recommendation.
- In 1985, was under investigation for the sale and possession of cocaine, along with Roger Clinton (the President's half-brother) who was being investigated for the purchase and use of cocaine. Earlier, gave Roger $8,000 to pay off drug debts he had accumulated.
  (NOTE: He later told the FBI that he distributed cocaine on more than 180 occasions. He stated "I shared my success in that manner".)
- In 1985, during the criminal investigation of Lasater, then-Governor Clinton awarded Lasater a $30.2 million bond issue to modernize the State police radio system. Lasater received $750,000 underwriting fee for the radio bond.
- In 1986, was sentenced to 2.5 years in prison, with Roger Clinton testifying against him. Although already in jail on cocaine possession charges, Roger Clinton was named an "unindicted" co-conspirator, charges

which would have carried a much stronger sentence than his then-current conviction. Lasater appealed and thus did not begin his sentence immediately. In 1990, Governor Clinton pardoned him.

- From 1984 to 1987, he owned a New Mexico resort called Angel Fire where alleged drug parties were held which Special Prosecutor Starr is also investigating.
- Lasater was sued by the FDIC for illegal activity involving failed S&Ls, and has been suspected of illegal bond running through Lasater & Co.

  (*NOTE*: *Dennis Patrick claims that in 1985 and 1986, Lasater & Co. traded nearly $60 million in bonds in Mr. Patrick's name without his knowledge.*)

  (SEE: Appendix D)

Lauramoore, John H. and Marylin B

Purchased a lot in Whitewater from Hillary Clinton

(SEE: Appendix A)

Leach, Jim

U.S. Representative R-IA

Chairman, Banking and Financial Services Committee

- Holding hearings on Whitewater, the death of Vince Foster, Mena drug running, money laundering and related matters.

  (SEE: Flowerwood, Vince Foster, Mena,

Whitewater, Barry Seal)

Lee, Henry Dr.

Forensic scientist who testified at the O.J. Simpson trial

- Hired by Whitewater prosecutors to examine the physical evidence and photos taken in the Foster death.

Lewis, Jean L.

Senior Criminal Investigator with the Kansas City, Missouri office of the Resolution Trust Corporation (RTC) until September 29, 1995.

- Sent criminal referrals outlining conspiracy and other crimes relating to Madison Guaranty Savings & Loan to the Justice Department.
- Among other things, the referrals "provided specific check numbers, dates, account names, account balances, particular uses of funds, and the names of individuals and entities involved in various check kiting schemes. The referrals also stated that among those who stood to benefit from this activity were Stephen Smith, Jim Guy Tucker, then-Governor Bill Clinton and Mrs. Clinton, Bill Clinton Political Committee Fund, James and Susan McDougal, Chris Wade, and several former Madison officers and borrowers... inasmuch as "the overdrafts and loan transactions, or alleged check 'swapping' and kiting between the combined companies' accounts ensured that loan payments and other corporate

obligations were met, thus clearly benefiting the principals of each entity."

- Placed on leave August 17, 1994.

(SEE: Appendix A, Whitewater, Paula Casey, Flowerwood, IDC, Jim McDougal, Web Hubbell, RTC, April Breslaw)

Lindsey, Bruce
Deputy White House Counsel
Treasurer of the 1990 Clinton presidential campaign

- Testified at the Whitewater hearings in January 1996
- Established that the Whitewater Development Corp. and the Madison Guaranty Savings & Loan were discussed during Arkansas-Texas Southern basketball game played in Fayetteville, Arkansas, Dec. 28, 1993.
- During the game, he spoke with former Arkansas State Securities Commissioner Beverly Bassett Schaffer in poultry magnate Don Tyson's box.

  (NOTE: Eight days before the basketball game, the president's handwritten notes questioned whether he could count on Mrs. Schaffer's support in the Whitewater investigation. Shortly after Governor Clinton named her in 1985, Schaffer approved a stock offering by the soon-to-be-bankrupt Madison S&L.)

  (SEE: Appendix A, Appendix B, "Skybox meeting")

Livingstone, Craig
Special Assistant to William Kennedy III

- Joined Kennedy in identifying Vince Foster's body at the morgue.

Lot 7 (Whitewater)

- Owned by Chris Wade but transferred title to the Lauramoores to shield the asset from the bankruptcy court when he filed for protection. He paid the Lauramoores $200 a week to hold the title for him, and there was a $60,105 loan in their name from Citizens Bank of Lavaca to build a house on the lot.

Lot 13 (Whitewater)

- In 1984 and 1985, the Clintons improperly claimed an interest deduction on a $30,000 loan used to build a modular home on lot 13 in Whitewater. (
  NOTE: *The Whitewater Corp. actually made the payments, and the Clintons corrected their taxes in 1993, paying over $4,000 in taxes and penalties.)*
- Sold to a Mississippi businessman who defaulted on his payments. Purchased by the Clintons from the bankruptcy trustee, and sold a month later to John and Marylin Lauramoore, reporting a $1,600 capital gain on their taxes. The transactions were handled by Hillary Rodham Clinton.
- Instead of making payments directly to Whitewater Corp., or to the Clintons, the Lauramoores paid some of the money into an escrow account belonging to Chris Wade's real estate company.
  *(**NOTE:** The Lauramoores paid $28,000 on a loan to Citizens Bank & Trust, repaying a loan for the home.)*

Lyons, James
Denver attorney

- Trusted figure in the Clinton inner circle since the early 1980s. Hired by Bill Clinton during the 1992 campaign.

- Issued the first audit of the Clintons' Whitewater involvement that claimed the couple lost $68,900. The "Lyons Report" — subsequently discredited by the New York Times' Jeff Gerth — helped quash stories of Whitewater irregularities for the remainder of the electoral race.

- Helped discredit claims of women alleging relationships with Bill Clinton during 1992 campaign.

- Between January 1993 and March 1994, Lyons left thirty-eight messages for Webster Hubbell, once calling from the White House, where he was a frequent visitor.

- Vince Foster was considering hiring Lyons to be his own attorney in the Travelgate scandal. On July 20, the day Foster died, Lyons left multiple messages for both Foster and Hubbell. He was scheduled to fly to Washington to meet with Foster the next day.

- Appointed by the Administration in October 1993 to a government advisory panel seeking peace in Ireland.

  (SEE: Appendix A)

Lyon, William

Mayor of Fordyce, AR

Head of the Lyon Folder Company

Former member of the Arkansas Banking Board

- Testified before the Whitewater Committee that James McDougal boasted to him that he had considerable influence with Clinton and his wife, Hillary Rodham Clinton while asking Lyon resign from the Banking Board. Upon his refusal to resign, Lyon testified he subsequently received a call from the-Governor Clinton and resigned at Clinton's request.

  (SEE: Appendix A)

M

Madison Guaranty Savings & Loan
Little Rock Arkansas savings and loan company

- Purchased in 1979 by James McDougal.
- Assets grew from $0.5 million in 1979 to $120 million in 1985
- Failed in 1989, at a cost of $60 million to taxpayers.
- Made a number of loans to Clinton friends and supporters which were not repaid.
- Held a number of important accounts including Whitewater Development Corp.'s checking account.
- 1985, McDougal hosted a fund-raiser at Madison for Clinton.
- Made over $1,000,000 in loans to companies controlled by Jim Guy Tucker.

    (*NOTE: Madison Guaranty Savings & Loan not to be confused with Madison Bank & Trust located in Augusta, Arkansas*)

    (SEE: Appendix A, Jim McDougal, Jim Guy Tucker, Whitewater Development Corp.)

Malak, Fahmy
Former Arkansas State medical examiner

- Was appointed to the post by then-governor Clinton

    (SEE: Appendix D, Kevin Ives)

Marks, William J., Sr

- Indicted June 7, 1995 along with John Haley on charges of conspiracy, wire fraud, bank fraud, mail fraud and misapplying funds.
- Pleaded not guilty.

Mathias, Robert
Former Federal prosecutor

- David Watkins' attorney who invoked House Committee Rule 3(f)(2)at Watkins' appearance before the House Government Reform and Oversight Committee (January 18, 1996), forcing TV cameras and microphones to be removed.

   (SEE: Appendix A)

Margolis, David
Associate Deputy Attorney General

- Gave Senate Whitewater Committee an account of events leading to the search of the office of Vince Foster that directly contradicted testimony of then-White House counsel Bernard Nussbaum. Said that he was instructed by Philip Heymann, the deputy attorney general, to go to the White House along with another Justice Department official to review the documents in Foster's office.
- Said Nussbaum reneged on an agreement to let Justice Dept. lawyers view the first pages of files found in Foster's office for any evidence as to why he might

have committed suicide, including possible evidence of extortion or blackmail.

(*NOTE: Nussbaum defended his conduct. Told the senators he had never made such an agreement with Margolis.*

(SEE: Appendix C)

Markland, Peter (Sgt.)
US Park Police detective

- 18 yr. veteran testified that he believes the White House hampered the investigation of Foster's suicide two years ago because it was trying to hide documents – – possibly about Whitewater. Also said he didn't believe the White House's explanation of why it took six days to find a handwritten note allegedly left by Foster.

(*NOTE: committee member Sen. John Kerry, D-Mass., said any suggestion that Nussbaum didn't simply overlook the NOTE is "just pure conjecture."*)

(SEE: Appendix C, Nussbaum, Foster)

Marshall, Capricia
Executive assistant to Hillary Rodham Clinton

- Had regular access to the room where the missing Rose billing records were found by Carol Huber.
- Testified in February 1996 before Washington Grand Jury regarding Hillary Clinton's missing billing records

(SEE: Billing Records, Carol Huber, David Kendall, Hillary Clinton, Whitewater, Seth Ward, Flowerwood)

Martens, Darnell
Businessman

- Wrote January 29,1993 memo to partner and Hollywood producer Harry Thomason suggesting ways Thomason could use his access to the new administration to secure "Washington opportunities" for their aviation consulting firm, TRM. The memo expressed interest in the White House travel office and a project to review the non-military government aircraft fleet.

  (SEE: Appendix B, Travelgate, Harry Thomason, Billy Dale)

Massey, Richard
Attorney and partner, Rose law firm

- Testified (January, 1996) before the Senate Whitewater Committee about Rose Law firm's representation of Madison Guaranty S&L.
- Since the 1992 presidential campaign, credited by Hillary Rodham Clinton as the person responsible for bringing the Madison account to Rose law firm. At the time, Massey was an associate at Rose, 8 months out of law school. Mrs. Clinton claimed Massey "did all the work" while she "just supervised".
- Massey's testimony directly contradicted almost everything Mrs. Clinton had to say about his involvement in the representation.

  (SEE: Madison Guaranty S&L, Rose law firm)

Master Marketing
Advertising, public relations and real estate firm controlled by Susan McDougal

- Borrowed $300,000 from Capital Management Services in 1986. No payments were ever made. The loan was illegal, and allegedly was made at the urging of then-Governor Bill Clinton
- Indicted along with Jim McDougal and Govenor Jim Guy Tucker for assorted business schemes. Trial scheduled to begin March 1996Matthew, Charles
- Indicted along with Eugene Fitzhugh and David Hale on a federal charge of conspiring to defraud the SBA.

  (SEE: Appendix A)

Matthew, Charles
- Indicted June 23, 1994 along with Eugene Fitzhough and David Hale on a federal charge of conspiring to defraud the SBA.

McCurry, Michael D.
White House press secretary

- Succeeded Dee Dee Myers

McDougal, Jim
Owner of Madison Guaranty Savings & Loan

- Met Bill Clinton in 1968 when they were both working on

the staff of Senator J. William Fulbright (D, Arkansas.)

- Madison failed in 1989 at a cost to taxpayers of at least $60 million.
- Clinton's economic development aide in his first term as governor.
- Clinton's partner in Whitewater Development Corporation.
- Owner of Kingston Bank & Trust.
- Had ties to The Cherry Valley Bank.
- Removed from Madison Guaranty by federal regulators in 1986.
- Acquitted of fraud in 1990.
- Filed for the Democratic primary on March 29, 1994 for the US House of Representatives.
- Currently under a 14-count indictment for assorted business schemes in Arkansas. Trial scheduled to begin March, 1996.

  (SEE: Appendix A, Bill Clinton, Hillary Clinton, Flowerwood Farms, David Hale, Madison Guaranty S&L, Seth Ward, Web Hubbell, Whitewater, Whitewater Development Corp.)

McDougal, Susan
Former wife of James McDougal

- Partner in Whitewater Development Corporation.
- Received a fraudulent $300,000 federally-backed loan from David Hale's Capital Management Services, allegedly at Governor Clinton's direction. Some of the money apparently was used to pay Whitewater

bills.

- Received over $1,500,000 from James McDougal's Madison Guaranty Savings & Loan from 1983 to 1986.
- After divorce, moved to Los Angeles, where she worked as a bookkeeper for conductor Zubin Mehta, who accused her of writing 300 unauthorized checks totaling approximately $200,000
  —February 9, 1995 **London Daily Telegraph**
- Questioned by prosecutors for the first time on February 8, 1995

McLarty, Thomas "Mac"
White House Chief of Staff

(SEE: Appendix A, Appendix C)

Media By-Pass
Magazine whose subtitle is "The Uncensored National News.".

- Published Jim Norman's "Fostergate" article after it was spiked by Forbes.

Mena, Arkansas
Location of Intermountain Airport, alleged base for Iran-Contra gun- and drug-running operations

(SEE: Appendix D)

Mills, Cheryl D.
Special assistant to then-White House counsel Abner Mikva

- Owner of car burglarized (July 13, 1995) in which "sensitive documents" were stolen, including ones pertaining to the investigation of the 1993 death Vince Foster and the 1994 federal raid on the Branch Davidian compound at Waco, Texas.
  (NOTE: Deputy White House press secretary Mary Ellen Glynn, confirming the break-in, said, " All those documents are replaceable".)

Morris, Roger
Former National Security Council staffer

- Along with former UPI investigative reporter Sally Denton wrote extensive article concerning drug running and money laundering in Mena, Arkansas based on files, papers mostly from Barry Seal.
- Article originally scheduled to be published in Washington Post but spiked by editor at the last minute allegedly due to pressure from CIA.
- It was subsequently published in Penthouse Magazine.

  (SEE: Appendix D, Sally Denton, Mena, Barry Seal)

N

Nash, Bob

Former president of ADFA, 1987 - 1991

Personnel Director of the White House

(SEE: Appendix D, ADFA, Coral Reinsurance)

NCEE

National Center on Education and the Economy

- New York state agency
- Being questioned by New York attorney general about $101,630 paid to Hillary Rodham Clinton just prior to the 1992 presidential campaign.
- NCEE says Mrs. Clinton "...met with educators, state lawmakers and other officials to "promote the agency's agenda" Payments to Mrs. Clinton are not reflected on the required federal forms that non-profit agencies like NCEE are required to submit. (NY Post)

    (*NOTE: Mrs. Clinton was appointed to the NCEE board of directors along with Ira Magaziner around 1991. She was the only member of the board of directors to be paid ($101,630) according to NCEE's president Marc Tucker, who released the information to the State Attorney General's office.*)

(SEE: Appendix A)

Neel, Roy
Deputy Chief of Staff at the time of Vince Foster's death.

> (NOTE: *The trash had been removed from Foster's office that night by a janitor. White House lawyers retrieved it that night and stored it for most of the next day in Neel's office.*)

(SEE: Appendix C)

Nichols, Larry
Marketing director, Arkansas Development Finance Authority. (ADFA)

- Discovered bond "irregularities" in the agency, and went to then-Governor Bill Clinton with his discoveries. Subsequently resigned and became outspoken critic of Clinton, appearing in videos ("The Clinton Chronicles") and on radio talk shows regarding Whitewater and other related subjects.

  (SEE: Appendix A, Appendix D, ADFA)

Norman, James R.
Former Forbes investigative reporter

- Senior editor at Forbes who was allegedly fired for pursuing the Foster story
- Wrote Forbes cover story entitled "Oil! Guns! Greed!"(January 1995.)...
- Eventually published "Fostergate," (August 1995, Media Bypass.)

  (SEE: Appendix C)

NSA
The National Security Agency

- Serves as arm of US intelligence, controlled by the Defense Dept. Has larger budget than the CIA.
- Chief function is to collect intelligence from satellites and by eavesdropping on telephone and computer traffic all over the world.

  (SEE: Appendix D)

Nussbaum, Bernard
Former chief White House counsel

- Resigned after improper contacts with the Treasury Department over the Whitewater investigation.
- Entered Vince Foster's office and removed files the night Foster's body was found at Ft. Marcy Park.
- Refused to allow investigators access to Foster's office for two days.
- Declared Mr. Foster's briefcase empty - four days before a ripped up note in Mr. Foster's handwriting was "discovered" in it.
- Insisted that White House lawyers be present during interviews with staff during the investigation into Foster's death, possibly discouraging a frank exchange of views.
- Met with Treasury officials regarding a Resolution Trust

Corporation investigation of Madison Guaranty S&L on September 29, 1993.

- Testified before Senate Whitewater Committee regarding his actions relating to his search of Vince Foster's office that he "had done nothing wrong".
- Subpoenaed to testify before a federal grand jury
- Resigned April 5, 1994

(SEE: Appendix A, Appendix C)

O

O'Neil, Henry P.
Secret Service agent

- Testified before the Senate Whitewater Committee that
  he saw Margaret Williams, Hillary Rodham
  Clinton's Chief of Staff, "carrying, in her arms and
  her hands, what I would describe as file folders,"
  from the office of Vince Foster the night of his death

  (SEE: Appendix A, Williams, Margaret)

Olson, Theodore
**Washington lawyer retained to represent David
Hale before the Senate Special Whitewater Com-
mittee**

- Worked with Whitewater independent counsel Kenneth
  Starr in President Reagan's Justice Department
- Was a party in Morrison vs. Olson, a U.S. Supreme Court
  case concerning the jurisdiction of independent
  counsel;

  (SEE: David Hale)

Orenstein Julian Dr.
**Physician on duty at the Emergency Room at Fairfax
Hospital**

- Certified death of Vince Foster.
- According to his FBI statement, he did not see an exit wound.
- Stated he lifted the body by the shoulders "to locate and observe the exit wound in the decedent's head." But he told the London Sunday Telegraph that this was not the case. "I never saw [an exit wound] directly."

  (SEE: Appendix C)

P

Palladino, Jack
San Francisco private investigator

- Hired by James Lyons during Bill Clinton's presidential campaign and then billed the campaign for Palladino's services.
- Lyons' law firm in turn paid Palladino's $28,000 fee. Palladino's work allegedly involved threatening and intimidating women not to go public with their stories about Clinton.

    (SEE: Appendix A, James Lyons)

Palmer, Robert
Owner, Palmer Properties, Inc.
Little Rock real estate appraiser

- Pleaded guilty (December 12, 1994) to conspiracy involving falsified real estate appraisals for Madison Guarantee Savings and Loan Association loans.
- Admitted to his involvement in covering up Madison's failure to follow a supervisory agreement with the Federal Home Loan Bank Board, which Madison had entered in 1984 after failing to keep adequate appraisal records for some real estate loans. He prepared 78 false and backdated appraisal to cover for loans that did not comply with the agreement, for which he received $15,350.

- The falsified and backdated appraisals involved Madison loans to Arkansas Governor Jim Guy Tucker, and David Hale.
- Crimes also included falsification of Madison records to deceive FHLBB examiners who were threatening to close down Madison.
- Sentenced on June 16, 1995 to 3 years probation and a $5,000 fine.

    (SEE: Madison Guarantee Savings & Loan, Jim McDougal, Whitewater, Jim Guy Tucker, David Hale, Bill Clinton.)

Park-O-Meter, Co.

Arkansas based parking meter manufacturing company owned by Seth Ward, Web Hubbell's father-in-law.

- Received loans from Governor Clinton's Arkansas Development Finance Agency (ADFA.)
- Web Hubbell drafted Act 1062, the piece of legislation creating ADFA
- First recipient of an AFDA loan
- Upon investigation, Park-O Meter was found also to have made retrofit nose cone compartments for airplanes allegedly used to haul cocaine in the Mena drug-smuggling operation. Further reports allege that POM also manufactured nose cones for missiles specifically designed for use in chemical warfare.

    (SEE: Appendix D, AFDA , Mena, Barry Seal, IDC, Hillary Clinton, Bill Clinton, Jim McDougal, Seth Ward, AFDA)

Parks, Gary
Son of Luther "Jerry" Parks

- Charged that his father was killed "to save Bill Clinton's political career...my dad was working on Clinton's infidelities for about six years, starting in the campaign around 1983," and had compiled two name-and-photo-filled files on Mr. Clinton that he kept hidden in his bedroom.

  —*London Telegraph*

  (**NOTE:** *Shortly before he was killed, Mr. Parks' Little Rock home was broken into. The phone lines were severed and the security system was dismantled. Jane Parks, Mr. Parks' widow, says the pair of Clinton files were missing and "must have been stolen.")*

(SEE: Luther "Jerry" Parks)

Parks, "Jerry" Luther
Owner of American Contract Services Inc.

- Provided security for Clinton's Presidential campaign and transition headquarters.
- Victim of a mob-style hit in Little Rock September 26, 1993.

  (**NOTE:** *In an interview with Ambrose Evans-Pritchard, the Parks family have accused Little Rock Police of orchestrating a cover-up after the detective on the case was removed. Mrs. Parks said that her husband has kept sensitive files on Mr. Clinton dating back to 1984. One concerned a series of drug parties allegedly attended by Governor Clinton. A second stemmed from work undertaken by Mr. Parks in 1987 involving night surveillance of the governor. Mrs. Parks alleges that the files were stolen in July 1993 in a well planned burglary that disabled the house's sophisticated alarm system. Mr. Parks was murdered two months later.")*

(SEE: Appendix D, Arkancide)

Patrick, Dennis
Former customer of Lasater & Co.

- Millions of dollars were run through his account (1985-86) without his knowledge or permission, despite repeated complaints to then executive vice-president Patsy Thomasson.
- Allegedly in the witness protection program.

  (SEE: AFDA, Dan Lasater, Patsy Thomasson)

Patterson, Larry
Arkansas State trooper

- In a legally binding deposition in a suit filed against Buddy Young, the former head of then-Governor Clinton's security detail, Patterson said Bill Clinton knew about illegal and extra-legal activities at Mena
- Said he had overheard conversations about "large quantities of drugs being flown into Mena airport, large quantities of guns, that there was an ongoing operation training foreign people in the area." When asked, "Were any of these conversations in the presence of Governor Bill Clinton?" he replied: "Yes, sir." .
- Patterson was being deposed in a legal suit filed against Buddy Young by Terry Reed.

  (SEE: Appendix D, Terry Reed, Mena)

Perdue, Sally
Former Miss Arkansas, talk show hostess

- Said in an interview with the London Sunday Telegraph that during her 1983 affair with Bill Clinton, he would smoke (and inhale) two or three marijuana cigarettes in a typical evening
- Made similar statements in a taped interview for Sally Jesse Raphael Show, however the show was never aired.

  (SEE: Troopergate)

Perry, Roger
Arkansas State Trooper

- Has signed a affidavit stating that he learned of the death of Vince Foster between 4:30 and 7 pm (CT) (Note: 5:30-8 pm Washington time — at least 30 mimutes before the US Park Police officially notified the White House.)
- Says he was on duty the afternoon at the governor's mansion in Little Rock when Chelsea Clinton's former nanny, Helen Dickey, called from the White House: "She was kind of hysterical, crying, real upset...She told me that Vince got off work, went out to his car in the parking lot, and shot himself in the head.".
- After receiving the call, Perry telephoned several other people in Little Rock to relay the news. One of them was Trooper Larry Patterson. Another was Lynn Davis, former commander of the Arkansas State Police. They have both issued affidavits swearing

that they learned about Foster's death around 6 PM Central Time, a full hour and a half before the official notification of the White House.

(SEE: Appendix C, Helen Dickey)

Perry County Bank
Located in Perryville, northwest of Little Rock

- Site of an account which held funds for Clinton's 1990 campaign.
- Loaned $180,000 to the 1990 Clinton campaign.
- Just before the 1990 primary (May 25, 1990), Clinton's campaign treasurer, Bruce Lindsey, withdrew $30,000 in cash. The president of the bank at the time, Neal Ainley, has been convicted for conspiring to hide the withdrawal from the IRS. (Note: Banks are required to report all transactions involving $10,000 or more, but Ainley removed the report for the transaction from the mail bin. Later told the FDIC that he had complied with the law.) Lindsey says that the withdrawal was used to fund "get-out-the-vote" activities among minorities. Following Clinton's 1990 victory, the co-owners of the bank were appointed to positions overseeing highway construction and banks.

Pittsburgh Tribune-Review
Pennsylvania newspaper that has broken many stories on Vince Foster's death

(SEE: Chris Ruddy)

93

Poor, Jesse
Installer, Atlantic X-Ray

- Provided records revealing that the X-ray machine used by Dr. James Beyer had been installed new on June 15, 1993 and the first service call was received on October 23, three months after the suicide.
  (NOTE: Dr. Beyer testified x-rays he had taken of Vince Foster had, in fact, not been taken because of the broken machine.)

  (SEE: Appendix C, Dr. James Beyer)

Presidential Legal Defense Trust

Official name of the fund set up to raise cash to cover the Clintons' bills arising from the numerous legal problems since taking office

PROMIS

Sophisticated tracking software developed by Inslaw

(SEE: Appendix D, Inslaw)

"Protocol"

Reportedly refers to a large load of private Clinton papers that was moved to Clinton/Gore headquarters in Little Rock in the dead of night in early fall 1995.

- Documents allegedly came from the basement of the First Commercial Bank building and the Worthen Bank building, both in Little Rock. Other documents were collected from the Rose Law Firm and Jennings & Bryan, the firm in which senior White House aide Bruce Lindsey was a partner.
- Transfer of the papers was organized by Betsey Wright, Bill Clinton's former Arkansas chief of staff.
- Investigators for Special Prosecutor Ken Starr believe the documents deal not only with the Clinton's Whitewater property investment. They also suspect papers detailing another land deal called Flowerwood are at Clinton/Gore headquarters along with files that could cast light on the first family's business relationships with the Arkansas firm Wal-Mart and with "chicken king" Don Tyson.

  (SEE: Flowerwood, Rose Law Firm, Don Tyson, Bruce Lindsey, Betsey Wright, Whitewater)

Psychiatrist (Foster)

- FBI report quotes an unnamed psychiatrist a who states that he was contacted by Foster's sister Sheila Anthony, explaining that Foster was working on "Top Secret" issues at the White House and "that his depression was directly related to highly sensitive and confidential matters." Allegedly, Foster needed assurances that nothing revealed in counseling sessions could be flushed out by subpoena at a later date. Four days later, the body of Vince Foster was found in Fort Marcy Park.

  (SEE: Vince Foster, Fostergate)

R

Raley's Towing
Company that towed Foster's car from Ft. Marcy Park to the Park Police headquarters

- According to the transcript of a taped telephone conversation at the time, a driver can be heard in the background saying that Foster's car was taken to the CIA:

    > "That would have gone to Park Police headquarters," said one of the staff, when asked about Foster's Honda.

    > "No, it went to the CIA and then went to headquarters," said the driver.

    > "Oh, it went to CIA first?"
    > (***NOTE***: *Raley's Towing refuses to elaborate, saying now it will divulge information only if compelled under a subpoena*)

    (SEE: Appendix C)

Reagan, Mike
Talk show host

- Has featured interviews with Larry Nichols, Terry Reed and others concerning Whitewater, the death of Vince Foster, Mena, etc.

Reed, Terry
Former Air Force intelligence operative

- Co-author with John Cummings of *"Compromised: Clinton, Bush and the CIA. An inside view of the inner workings of the Iran-Contra affair and the resulting Whitewater scandal"*.
- Plaintiff in a civil-rights suit against Buddy Young.
- Trained Contra pilots, under Barry Seal's supervision, at Nella, Ark.

    (SEE: Appendix D, Barry Seal, Buddy Young, Mena, Don Lasater, Larry Patterson, L.D. Brown)

Reeves, Robert
"Mayor of Ft. Marcy Park"

- Outside observer who had spent many hours in the Park prior to Vince Foster's death. (He considers the park a "second home".)
- Believes Foster's body was found by the first cannon — in contradiction to the Fiske report.

    (SEE: Appendix C, Vince Foster, Ft. Marcy Park, Fiske Report)

Reno, Janet
U.S. Attorney General

- Appointed Robert Fiske, first Special Prosecutor to investigate Whitewater and the death of Vince Foster.

Rolla, John
U.S. Park Police Investigator

- Lead investigator at death scene of Vince Foster in Ft. Marcy Park, in his first supervisory role.

    (SEE: Appendix C)

Rose Law Firm
Little Rock, Arkansas legal firm

- Many of the people involved in the Whitewater scandal, including a number of administration officials, were (or are) lawyers at the Rose Law Firm. The firm was also involved in some of the lawsuits concerning Madison Guaranty. Specifically, they represented the government in suing the S&L, with Webster Hubbell as the supervising attorney.
- A number of files with Vince Foster's initials on them were allegedly shredded at the law firm shortly after the special prosecutor was appointed. Rose has filed suit against the RTC in order to keep their client list confidential.

    (*NOTE: The RTC needs the list to determine if Rose was involved in a conflict of interest when they represented the RTC.*)
- A full list of members and major clients was found in the Martindale-Hubble directory:

Major **Rose** clients **(Whitewater associated entities in bold)**:
    Axciom Corporation, Aluminum Corporation of America, Arkansas Association of Bank Holding Companies, Arkansas Freightways, Arkansas Poultry Federation, Arkansas-Okla-

homa Gas Corporation (ARKLA), **Beverly Enterprises**, Bridgestone/Firestone Inc., Canon Express Inc., The Equitable Life Assurance Society of the United States, Fairfield Communities Inc., Federal Deposit Insurance Corporation, General American Transportation, General Electric, General Motors, Georgia-Pacific, The John Hancock Mutual Life Insurance Co., Harps Food Stores, Harvest Foods, International Paper, The Kemper Insurance Group, Massachusetts Mutual Life Insurance, MCI Telecommunications, 3M, New York Life Insurance Co., Paine-Webber, Panhandle Eastern Corporation, Pel-Freeze Inc., The Prudential Insurance Company of America, J. A. Riggs Tractor, The Winthrop Rockefeller Foundation, **Stephens Inc.**, **Systematics Information Services**, TCBY, Tramell Crow Companies, **Tyson Foods Inc.**, USX Corporation, Wal-Mart Stores Inc., WEHCO Media Inc., **Worthen Banking Corporation**

(SEE: Appendix A, Appendix C, Appendix D)

Rodriguez, Miguel
Former prosecutor for Special Prosecutor Ken Starr

- Resigned, reportedly due to interference from Ken Starr's Deputy Independent Counsel Mark Tuohey in that he was prevented from pursuing critical leads. Reportedly, Tuohey made it clear to him that he favored a quick ruling of suicide. Rodriguez responded that he wasn't going to be part of a cover-up, according to an article in the Pittsburgh Tribune-Review.

RTC (Resolution Trust Corporation)

Established to investigate failed federally insured Savings and Loan companies

- In March 1992, began an investigation of possible criminal activity at Madison after the New York Times published a major story about the Whitewater Development Corp.

- September 1992, the RTC sent a criminal referral, criminal investigation request to the Justice Department urging a thorough investigation of a "check kiting scheme" in which over $100,000 in Madison funds were alleged to have been illegally funneled into the Whitewater Development Corp. President and Mrs. Clinton were named as potential beneficiaries of this scheme.

- September 1993, RTC sent a second criminal referral to the Justice Department regarding Madison Guaranty. This referral contained nine specific allegations of criminal wrongdoing. The second referral named President and Mrs. Clinton as possible witnesses.

  (SEE: Appendix A, Jean Lewis, Paula Casey, Whitewater Development Corporation, Web Hubbell.)

Rubin, Robert

Secretary of the Treasury

Director of the National Economic Council

Former president of Goldman Sach's Investment Bank

- Succeeded former Treasury Secretary Lloyd Bentsen

    (SEE: Appendix D, Lloyd Bentsen)

Ruddy, Christopher

Investigative reporter—Pittsburgh Tribune-Review

- Premiere reporter in American press who broke the original set of stories in the New York Post in January and February 1994 that revealed a possible cover-up in the death of Vince Foster.
- Apparently forced to leave the New York Post for his interest in pursuing Foster death anomalies.
- Target of a "deconstruction", a questioning of his credibility during an interview with Mike Wallace for "60 Minutes" that dealt with the Foster suicide.

    (SEE: Appendix C)

S

SBA
Small Business Administration

Santucci, Fred and Scalice, Vincent
NYPD homicide detectives (retired), who performed their own two month investigation into the Foster (1995.)

- Issued a report concluding that the crime scene had "likely been staged," with the gun placed in Foster's hand to make it look like a suicide and "a high probability exists that Foster's body was transported to Fort Marcy Park."
  (**NOTE**: *This report was funded by the Western Journalism Center in California*)

Schaffer, Beverly Bassett
Head of the Arkansas State Securities Department

- Appointed January 1985 by then-Governor Bill Clinton, allegedly at the request of Jim McDougal.
- Served as a lawyer for Madison Guaranty S&L.
- Allowed Madison Guaranty to operate while virtually insolvent for 18 months.

(NOTE: Alleged to have been accomplished by hiring a former Madison employee to run the state audit of Madison Savings and who reported that the institution was sound. The auditor was eventually indicted for mishandling the audit..)

- Husband is a corporate attorney for Tyson Foods, and was involved in arranging Hillary Clinton's successful futures trades.

  (SEE: Appendix A, Cattlegate, Madison Guaranty S&L, Jim McDougal, Tyson Foods.)

Scott, Marsha

White House liaison to the gay and lesbian community.

- Became known as "Bill's hippie girlfriend".
- Vince Foster's secretary told the FBI Foster had an "unusual" closed-door meeting in his office with Scott on July 19, 1993 — the day before his death. Told FBI she couldn't remember what they discussed.
- Quoted in the Fiske Report as saying Foster told her he had come to "a decision."
- Before and after that meeting, Scott called Hubbell at his office.
- After Hubbell's guilty plea in December 1994, Scott and Bruce Lindsey helped Hubbell's wife Suzanna land a $59,022-a-year job in the Department of the Interior.

  (SEE: Robert Fiske, Fiske Report, Webster Hubbell, Bruce Lindsey)

Seal, Barry
Pilot, gun runner, drug smuggler, DEA informant

(SEE: Appendix D, Mena)

Seligman, Nicole
Lawyer in Williams & Connolly (David Kendall's firm)

- Subpoenaed to appear before the Grand Jury in the matter of Hillary Clinton's mysteriously re-appearing Rose billing records

   (SEE: Billing Records, Hillary Clinton, Flowerwood, David Kendall, Seth Ward, Whitewater)

Senate Whitewater Hearings

- On May 17, 1995, the Senate passed (96-3) a resolution calling for wide-ranging Whitewater hearings by a special committee headed by U.S. Senator Alphonse D'Amato (R-NY). Topics include Clinton's 1990 gubernatorial campaign and the removal of papers from Vince Foster's office following his death.

   (SEE: Appendix A)

Seper, Jerry
Reporter, Washington Times

- Washington Times "point man" on Whitewater, Vince

Foster and related stories.

Sessions, William (Judge)
Former FBI Director

- Despite his announced intention to resign after the confirmation of new director-designate Louis Freeh, Sessions was abruptly fired by Bill Clinton July 19, 1993, the day before death of Vince Foster.
- Charged that his firing the day before Foster's death led to a "compromised" investigation of the case.

  (SEE: Appendix C)

Sharman, Jackson R. III
Special counsel to the House Banking Committee for its investigation of Madison Guaranty and Whitewater.

Shehand, Michael J.
Head of the Office of Professional Responsibility at the Justice Department

- Author of July 24 memo to associate deputy attorney general David Margolis.

Shelton, Bill,

Arkansas police officer

Boyfriend of Kathy Ferguson

- Found dead on the grave of Mrs. Ferguson June 12, 1994 with a suicide note next to the body. A bullet had entered behind his right ear.

  —*The Economist*

  (SEE: Arkancide, Kathy Ferguson, John Walker, Paula Jones, Danny Ferguson)

Sherburne, Jane

Special White House counsel to the Clintons on Whitewater matters

- Subpoenaed to appear before the Grand Jury (January, 1996) in the matter of the Hillary Clinton's mysteriously re-appearing Rose billing records found by Carol Huber

Simonello, Peter

Park Police Technician

- Responsible for removing the gun which Foster reportedly held in his right hand, although he was left-handed.

  (SEE: Appendix C)

Skolnick, Sherman
Private investigator from Chicago

- Directs a "citizen's committee against government corruption" and once ran a local cable talk show.

"Skybox meeting"
Meeting allegedly held at Tyson Foods skybox at a University of Arkansas basketball game Dec. 28, 1993.

- Allegedly occurred a week after Clinton sent a note to aide Bruce Lindsey asking whether one of the Arkansas figures in the Whitewater saga, former state securities commissioner Beverly Bassett Schaffer, would continue to be helpful to the White House.
- Bruce Lindsey said Clinton was at the game in Fayetteville that evening but may not have been in the Tyson Foods skybox with him when Lindsey asked Archie Schaffer, a Tyson Foods Inc. official, whether his wife (Beverly Bassett Schaffer) would continue to defend the integrity of Hillary Clinton's work for Madison. Lindsey told the committee that Schaffer had said his wife was reluctant to defend the Clintons in the press because she felt reporters had distorted her actions and she felt she had been "stalked" by a TV camera crew.

  (SEE: Appendix A)

Sloan, Clifford
White House lawyer and aide to Bernard Nussbaum

- On the evening after Foster's death, returned a bag of garbage previously removed by janitors.

    (SEE: Appendix C)

Smaltz, Donald
Independent counsel investigating resigned Agriculture Secretary Mike Espy

> **(SEE: Appendix D, Tyson Foods, Inc., Joseph Henrickson)**

Smith, Stephen
Clinton's Chief of Staff when Clinton was the Arkansas Attorney General (1978-79)

Assistant during Clinton's first gubernatorial term.

- In the early 80s, jointly owned the Bank of Kingston with James McDougal.
- On 8 June 1995, pleaded guilty to one misdemeanor for making false claims in obtaining a $65,000 SBA loan from Capital Management Services, Inc. in a plea bargain agreement. The loan was supposed to be used for the development of a demographic research company, but instead was apparently used to pay off debt on the Kings River Land Co. development, which Smith, his father, Jim Tucker, and James McDougal owned.

- Little Rock associate of Bill Clinton and Jim Guy Tucker who has pleaded guilty to receiving a fraudulent SBA loan.

    (SEE: Appendix A, Bank of Kingston, Capital Management Services, Jim Guy Tucker, James McDougal)

Sprunt, Hugh
Private tax attorney

- Independently analyzed all 2,726 pages of testimony and documents collected in the official Foster investigation and released by the U.S. Senate in early 1995. His analysis, based entirely upon the official documentary record, compiled by the United States Senate, concludes that the verdict of suicide is remote from the facts.
- Wrote, compiled and published comprehensive 165-page "Citizen's Independent Report," for the "primary use of the members and staff of the special Senate Whitewater Committee."

    (SEE: Appendix C)

Starr, Kenneth
Independent Whitewater prosecutor

- Appointed by a three-judge panel August 5, 1994 to

replace Robert Fiske in investigating the Whitewater affair.

Background/qualifications:

- Federal appeals court judge
- Solicitor General of the United States
- Runs the appellate division of a prominent law firm

    (SEE: Appendix A, Appendix B, Appendix C, Appendix D)

Stephens, Jay

Former Republican federal prosecutor

- Object of White House aide George Stephanopoulos' ire when he learned Stephens was hired to handle possible civil suits growing out of the failure of Madison Guaranty S&L

    (SEE: Appendix A)

Stephens Inc.

Little Rock investment bank

- One of the largest U.S. investment banks outside New York
- Before ADFA, dominated the Arkansas municipal bond underwriting market.
    (NOTE: The creation of ADFA reduced the dominance of Stephens Inc. to the benefit of firms such as Lasater & Co. that underwrote $664 million in Arkansas bond issues before Lasater was arrested on cocaine charges.)

    (SEE: Jackson Stephens, Rose Law Firm)

Strategic Investment
Investment newsletter and commentary

- Published several investigative and opinion articles about inconsistencies surrounding the investigation of Vince Foster's death.
- Commissioned a panel of handwriting experts to examine the Foster suicide note.
  (NOTE: Based upon analysis of three national document certification experts, the panel concluded the note was a forgery)

  (SEE: Appendix C, James Dale Davidson)

Steiner, Josh E.,
Former Treasury Department chief of staff

- Involved in contacts with the White House regarding Madsion Guaranty S&L.
- Resigned under firestorm of criticism after claiming on televised hearings that he lied to his diary.

Stephanopoulos, George
Senior adviser to the President

- Made news in March 1994 by acknowledging getting angry at the hiring of former Republican prosecutor Jay Stevens in connection with the Whitewater investigation.
  (NOTE: Stephens was hired to handle possible civil suits growing out of the failure of Madison Guaranty S&L, a thrift tied to the Whitewater land deal involving the Clintons.)
- Along with Harold Ickes, called a ranking Treasury

Department official to express outrage that Stephens, a critic of Clinton, had been retained.

- Told CNN he was "just trying to get information" but admitted to throwing a temper fit during the call.

  (SEE: Appendix A)

Stephens, Jackson

- Arkansas investment banker and bond trader
- Started Systematics, a Little Rock software sales and distributing company which was one of a number of companies involved in installing, selling, supporting, customizing and managing Promis software and bank data center operations;

  (SEE: Appendix D, Coral Reinsurance, Inslaw, Sytematics, Worthen Bank)

Stephens Security Bank

- April 3, 1985, lent $135,000 to James and Susan McDougal for Flowerwood Farms, a real estate development in western Pulaski County. Until 1984 more than 80 percent of its stock was owned by First Arkansas Bankstock Corp., the predecessor to the Worthen Banking Corporation.
- Some corporate matters were handled by C. Joseph Giroir, Jr.,chairman of the Rose Law Firm, who hired Hillary Clinton in 1978.

  *(**NOTE**: Investigators for several agencies now believe Hillary Clinton gave her personal backing to the McDougal loan, either as co-signer or guarantor.This was first reported by New York Post's John Crudele in May 1995.)*

112

- There had been earlier reports that a former senior vice president at Madison, Don Denton, had seen Hillary's name as guarantor on the back of a loan document in McDougal's loan file. The Wall Street Journal reported (August 1994) Denton told the staff of the independent counsel that he had seen her name, signed "Hillary Rodham," on a loan of between $100,000 and $300,000 in 1986, but that the usual form for a guarantee was missing. According to an article in "The American Spectator" : "At the time of the article, Clinton lawyer David Kendall issued the memorable but partial denial, "Any allegation that Mrs. Clinton guaranteed a loan in 1986 with the signature 'Hillary Rodham' has the unmistakable and clanging ring of falsity." (The loan would have been signed in 1985, not 1986.)
- More recently, however, Denton's memory has freshened, and he has reportedly given an affidavit to Independent Counsel Kenneth Staff stating that he was in the room when Hillary signed the loan. The April 3, 1985 note was secured by eleven lots in Flowerwood Farms, and the proceeds went into the Flowerwood Farms account at Madison Guaranty." —*The American Spectator, March 1996*

  (SEE: Appendix A, Flowerwood Farms)

Stewart, Amy
Attorney, Rose Law Firm in Little Rock, Ark.

- House guest of the Clintons for three straight weeks after her arrival in Washington on May 10, 1993.
- Trusted associate of Hillary Clinton and had been a

regular caller to Webster Hubbell's office. During her time at the White House she evidently worked out of Vince Foster's office, leaving Foster's number in her messages for Hubbell with whom she met on both May 20 and May 25, 1993.

(SEE: Appendix A)

Strayhorn, Susan

Secretary to Jim McDougal in the 1980's
Questioned by Whitewater independent counsel Ken Starr February 1, 1996 called as a witness before the Senate Whitewater looking into Hillary Clinton's role in a project involving a series of land deals later found by examiners to have been fraudulent.

(SEE: Appendix A, Billing Records, Hillary Clinton, Castle Gate, Jim McDougal, Madison Guarantee S&L)

Swann, Francis

Maintenance worker at Fort Marcy park

- As "CW" was leaving the park, he stopped Swann and co-worker Chuck Stough to tell them about the body he had just found. Swann called 911 to report the incident.

- Swann now disputes the transcript of the call as inaccurate: He was only aware of the one cannon while the police transcript says that he mentions the second.

    (SEE: Appendix A, "CW")

Systematics
Little Rock software sales and distributing company

- One of a number of companies involved in installing, selling, supporting, customizing and managing PROMIS software and bank data center operations.
- Founded by Jackson Stephens, Arkansas investment banker and bond trader.
- Grew rapidly in the 1970s as it took out more domestic business. In 1982, as the federal government was looking for a company to help out with the "Follow the Money" program, Systematics took on a big role and business boomed.
- Vince Foster and Webster Hubbell both owned stock in and provided legal services for the company

    (SEE: Appendix D, Inslaw)

T

Thomasses, Susan

Attorney, personal friend of Hillary Rodham Clinton

- Present either in person or via telephone at many questioned events relating to the Whitewater controversy
- Was at the White House for six hours the day seven travel employees were fired.
- Conferred with numerous White House figures including Hillary Rodham Clinton in Little Rock the night of Foster's death when files and documents were removed from Mr. Foster's office.
- Conferred with Hillary Clinton and then-Counsel Bernard Nussbaum, prior to Nussbaum refusing to allow Justice Department officials to participate in a review of documents in the Foster office.
- In the White House residence at the time Clinton attorney Robert Barnett arranged to take custody of "personal" Clinton papers retrieved from Foster's office and kept in the residence after Nussbaum's solitary review.
- Testified before Senate Whitewater Committee she didn't remember if she saw Hillary Rodham Clinton during several hours in the White House residence the week after Foster's death.

(SEE: Appendix C, Travelgate)

Thomason, Harry

Hollywood producer who made the celebrated " Man from Hope " convention film about Bill Clinton.

- Married to sit-com producer Linda Bloodworth-Thomason.
- Owned a one-third stake in TRM, a company that he tried to get in on the business of transporting the White House press corps accompanying the president.
- Subsequently hired Washington lawyer Bob Bennett to represent him.

    (SEE: Appendix A, Travelgate)

Thomasson, Patsy

Deputy director of the White House personnel office

- Formerly reported to David Watkins
- Appointed by then-Governor Clinton to the Arkansas Highway Commission.
- Worked for (Dan) Lasater Co. (later renamed to Phoenix in 1991) from 1980-1992.
- In 1985, acting as Vice President of the company, hired Roger Clinton as the company's limo driver at the request of then-Governor Clinton.
- In 1986, Lasater and Roger Clinton were both charged with the sale, purchase, and use of cocaine, and Patsy took over as president of the company.
- Under investigation by the SEC for illegal insider trading,

117

along with the uncle of William Kennedy. The trading was related to a Tyson acquisition target.

- Entered Vince Foster's office (along with Bernard Nussbaum on at least one occasion) the night of Foster's death and on at least two separate occasions, removing possible evidence.
  (Testified before a House committee on March 22, 1994 that she entered only once.)
- Allegedly switched personal computers with the one in Foster's office.
- Allegedly accessed Foster's safe and instructed the General Services Administration to move it out of the office.

(SEE: Appendix C)

Travelgate

Reference to an affair involving the abrupt firing of White House Travel Office employees

- On May 19, 1993 David Watkins fired Travel Office chief Billy Dale and six colleagues simultaneously, citing a host of financial irregularities and calling in the FBI to investigate.
- Five of the seven were later reinstated and given other government jobs.
- Four White House aides were subsequently reprimanded after an internal review headed by then-Chief of Staff Mack McLarty for making improper contacts with the FBI.
- Travel office chief Dale was charged with embezzling $68,000 from news organizations which reimbursed the travel office for the expense of flying their re-

porters around with the president. He was subsequently acquitted of all charges (December 1995)

(SEE: Appendix B, David Watkins, Harry Thomason, Catherine Cornelius, Susan Thomasses, Hillary Clinton)

Troopergate
Broad nickname given to revelations of alleged extramarital affairs of Bill Clinton

- A 1994 David Brock article in "The American Spectator" detailed the stories of Arkansas State Troopers Larry Patterson, Roger Perry, Danny Ferguson, Ronnie Anderson and L.D. Brown, who claim to have escorted then-Governor Bill Clinton on various liaisons as revealed in a law suit against Clinton filed by Larry Nichols.

  (NOTE: Critics claim Clinton's escapades are significant because many of the alleged affairs were carried out while the troopers were being paid public monies. The same critics also contend Clinton's lovers received lucrative state or national jobs in exchange for their silence.)

  (SEE: L.D. Brown, Danny Ferguson, Paula Jones, Larry Nichols, Roger Perry, The American Spectator, Buddy Young)

Tucker, Jim Guy
Governor of Arkansas

- Graduated from Harvard (1964.) University of Arkansas Law School (1968.)
- Ark. attorney general (1973-77.)

- Elected to Congress 1976.
- Defeated by Clinton for governor of Arkansas in 1982.
- Successful cable TV businessman while maintaining law practice.
- In 1990, Tucker was elected as Arkansas' lieutenant governor, and replaced Clinton as governor in 1992. *(NOTE: alleged to have asked state troopers L.D. Brown and Larry Patterson for compromising information on Clinton's private life in 1990, when Tucker was contemplating running for governor. Alleged to have retaliated against Brown by demoting him from white-collar investigations to highway patrol after Brown went public with information.)*
- Indicted June 7, 1995 on three felony charges for making false claims in obtaining $300,000 in loans from Capital Management Services, Inc. in 1987. He and his partner in a Florida cable television business, William J. Marks, claimed that the money was for a small Arkansas cable TV venture in order to qualify for the SBA loan. Instead, according to the indictment, it was used as collateral to obtain an $8,500,000 line of credit for a Florida cable TV business. Related charges involving shielding of assets from the IRS and false bankruptcy filings were also filed. His partner William J. Marks and John Haley, Tucker's personal lawyer, were also indicted.
- Allegedly received a phone call at his office notifying him of Vince Foster's death at least 30 minutes before the White House was officially notified.
- Named by the RTC in the criminal referrals for which Congress held hearings in August of 1994.

(SEE: Appendix A, Appendix C, Appendix D)

Tucker Sewer & Water Services

- In 1986, Jim Guy Tucker, the present Governor of Arkansas, made a proposal to provide water and sewer services to Castle Grande, a mobile-home park in Little Rock being being developed and financed by Jim McDougal's Madison Guaranty Savings and Loan.

  (*NOTE*: *Madison S&L loaned Tucker $860,000 on which he defaulted when Castle Grande failed. David Hale's Capital-Management Services loaned Tucker $300,000 on which he also defaulted.*)

- Castle Grande failed at a cost of $3.8 million to taxpayers
- Madison S&L failed at a cost of more than $60 million to the taxpayers
- Capital Management Services failed at a cost of $3.4 million to the taxpayers

  (SEE: Castle Grande, Capital Management Services, David Hale, Madison Guaranty S&L, Jim Guy Tucker)

Tyrell, Emmett R. Jr.
Editor-in-Chief, *The American Spectator*

Tyson, Don
Owner of Tyson foods, largest producer and distributor of chicken in the world.

  (SEE: Appendix A)

U

U.S. Park Police

- Given primary jurisdiction for the investigation of the death of Vice Foster despite FBI legal responsibility to investigate any death of one of top 25 presidential associates.

(SEE: Appendix C, Fostergate)

V

ValuePartners I

Fund in which the Clintons invested, managed by Smith Capital Management of Little Rock, Arkansas

- During the 1993 health care debate, in which Hillary Clinton was critical of drug companies, ValuePartners sold short in health-care stocks. The fund profited $275,000 from the transaction.
  *(**NOTE**: Clintons didn't set up a blind trust for their investments until July 1993.)*

  (SEE: Appendix A)

W

Wade, Chris
Owner, Ozark's Realty

- Real estate agent who managed Whitewater Development Corp.
- Purchased 24 Whitewater lots, 1985
- Collected payments and made deposits at Citizens Bank of Flippin. Stated that the venture did not lose money.
- Stated that "tens of thousands of dollars were passing through Whitewater's account" and that "the transactions seemed to bear no direct connection to Whitewater's lot sales or home development activity."
- March 19, 1995 pleaded guilty to two bankruptcy-related felony charges brought by Starr
- Concealed property holdings from a bankruptcy court.
- Owned property in the Whitewater development under another name.
- Admitted to receiving a loan based on a fraudulent application and hiding Flippin to buy the Whitewater property.

  (**NOTE:** *Reportedly, neither institution required financial statements from the Clintons. McDougal later acquired another $20,000 loan with which he paid off the original loan, freeing the Clintons from personal liability on it.*)
- Paid John H. and Marylin B. Lauramoore to hold property for him in their name.

(SEE: Appendix A)

Walker, John
Resolution Trust Corp. investigator working on Whitewater

- Allegedly jumped from the Lincoln Towers Building.

Walters, Gary
White House Chief Usher

- Former uniformed Secret Service officer; was assigned to first-family duty in 1970
- Joined the residential staff as an assistant usher in 1976, became chief usher in 1986.
- Subpoenaed along with Hillary Rodham Clinton and 5 others by Ken Starr to appear before the grand jury concerning the questionable re-appearance of Hillary Clinton's Rose Law Firm billing records in the White House residence "book room".
- As chief usher, reportedly kept a log of people entering and leaving the book room
- Supervises 89 employees responsible for the care and maintenance of the White House

  (SEE:

  (SEE: Appendix A, Billing Records, Hillary Rodham Clinton, Carol Huber, Rose Law Firm, Kenneth Starr, Whitewater)

Ward, Seth

Owner of Park-O-Meter (POM)

Officer of a Madison Guaranty S&L subsidiary

- Received $1,500,000 in loans from Madison.
- Defaulted on $587,793.
- Webster Hubbell's father-in-law
- Cited by Federal authorities as straw man purchaser in Castle Grande scam

  (SEE: Appendix A, Appendix D, Park-O-Meter, IDC, Castle Grande)

Watkins, David

Former Little Rock advertising executive

Former manager of Worthen Bank

Former assistant to President Clinton for management and administration

- Handled the firing of White House Travel Office chief Billy Dale and six White House travel office employees, trying to replace them with personnel from World Wide Travel, a Worthen Bank subsidiary.
- Author of 1993 memo to rebut criticisms of his actions in Travelgate, written to then-Chief of Staff Thomas F. "Mac" McLarty and implicating Hillary Clinton in the Travelgate scandal:
  "First Lady desired action - the action desired was the firing of the travel office staff...[and]...there'd be hell to pay if, after our failure in the Secret Service situation earlier, we failed to take swift and decisive

126

action in conformity with the First Lady's wishes." The memo was written in reference to her alleged interest in turning the travel office over to Harry Thomason.

- Accused of sexual harassment by a Clinton campaign worker.
- Left White House after being photographed using a military helicopter to play a round of golf at a New Market, MD. country club in 1994.
- Invoked House Committee Rule 3(f)(2) at his appearance before the House Government Reform and Oversight Committee, forcing TV cameras and microphones to be removed. (January 18, 1996)

(SEE: Appendix B, Travelgate, Billy Dale, Thomas "Mac" McLarty, Hillary Clinton, Harry Thomason, Patsy Thomasson.)

Welch, Russell
Arkansas state police investigator who has looked extensively at activities at Mena

(SEE: Appendix D, Barry Seal, Iran-Contra, Mena)

"Whitewater"
Reference to activities surrounding a Clinton real estate investment

- Started as a land development of riverfront property in Arkansas in 1980. The Clintons received a large share of the development without putting up any money. When the development went sour, additional capital infusions were needed. There is evidence and testimony suggesting that these cash infusions were obtained illegally from the Federal Government and never repaid.

(SEE: Appendix A, Jim McDougal, David Hale, Madison Guaranty S&L)

Whitewater Development Corporation

- Whitewater Development Corporation was formed in 1979 by James and Susan McDougal and Bill and Hillary Clinton. It was responsible for developing the 230 acres along the White River that the four had purchased the year before for about $200,000. The last Whitewater lots were sold in the spring of 1985. (Washington Post)

  (SEE: Appendix A, Jim McDougal, David Hale, Madison Guaranty S&L)

Wilcher, Paul

Attorney

- Allegedly investigating "The Octopus" found dead July 23, 1993, three days after Vince Foster.

  (SEE: Appendix D, Inslaw, Danny Casolaro)

Willis, Carol
Democratic National Committee

- One of the people involved in distributing cash to black ministers in Clinton's 1990 Gubernatorial campaign.

Williams, Margaret "Maggie"
Chief of Staff - Hillary Rodham Clinton

- According to Secret Service officer Henry P. O'Neil, Williams was seen carting files from Vincent Foster's office the night he died. She denied this in testimony before the Senate Whitewater Committee.
- Also denied telling an intern the papers he was carrying had come from Mr. Foster's office and needed to be reviewed by Hillary Rodham Clinton

  (SEE: Appendix C)

Woods, Henry (Judge)
U S District Judge hearing the case against Gov. Jim Guy Tucker, Jim and Susan McDougal

World Wide Travel
Little Rock travel agency that handled Clinton-Gore campaign travel arrangements in 1992

- Slated to take over White House Travel Office responsibilities in the wake of May 1993 firings by David Watkins.

- A Worthen Bank subsidiary

  (SEE: Appendix A, Travelgate, David Watkins, Worthen Bank)

Worsham, Sarah J.
Former FHLBB examiner

- Authored the 1984 report on Madison Guaranty Savings and Loan stating that it had engaged in "unsound lending practices" and stood "on the verge of insolvency".
- Went to work for the thrift one year later, hired by Jim McDougal, as a senior vice president at $65,000 a year, along with a $500-a-month expense allowance, yearly bonuses of $2,000 and a Bentley automobile.
- Served as a member of the Madison Guaranty S&L management committee, which oversaw loans. (Washington Times)

  (SEE: Appendix A, Jean Lewis, Jim McDougal, RTC, Whitewater)

Worthen Bank
Arkansas bank, subsidiary of Stephens Inc.

- Owner of World Wide Travel

  (SEE: Travelgate, David Watkins, World Wide Travel)

Wright, Betsey
Clinton White House aide

Former Arkansas chief of staff for then-Governor Bill Clinton

- Coined the phrase "bimbo eruptions" during the 1992 presidential campaign referring to women who were alleging sexual involvement(s) with candidate Clinton.
- Reportedly organized "Protocol"

    (SEE: "Protocol")

Wright, Susan (Judge)
Judge hearing the Paula Jones sexual harassment complaint against Bill Clinton (filed May 8, 1994)

Y

Young, Raymond "Buddy"

Head of the Federal Emergency Management Administration in Denton, Texas

Former head of then-Governor Clinton's Arkansas security detail.

- Defendant in civil suit filed by Terry Reed which alleges that Young attempted to frame him for insurance fraud;

  *(**NOTE**: Case#LR-C-94-634 is scheduled to go to trial in Arkansas mid-1996)*

  (SEE: Terry Reed)

Zupperman, Rose

Freelance make-up artist

- Testified in Fiske Report that at approximately 8:45pm, July 20, 1993 she overheard White House aide tell Presdent Clinton about a note retreived from Vince Foster's office.

  *(**NOTE**: Clinton has maintianed he wasn't aware of Foster's death until approximately 10pm, after his appearance on Larry King Live.)*

  (SEE: Appendix C)

APPENDICES

If nothing else has been firmly established, "Whitewater" and all of its ugly roots and branches have proven to be complex, convoluted, bungles in the jungle of business, law and politics. As noted elsewhere, much information about these sordid affairs has been available through various media outlets, both print and broadcast, for years. Unfortunately, for a variety of reasons, these places aren't frequented by most people.

Newspapers like The London Sunday Telegraph, the Pittsburgh Times-Review, Investors Business Daily, magazines like Media Bypass, Insight, The Weekly Standard and The American Spectator and newsletters like AIM and Strategic Investment and others are not publications that, despite generous subscription offers, grace the coffee tables of American homes everywhere. While Time, Newsweek, and US News and World Report have greater popularity, circulation and influence, collectively they haven't given as much coverage to Whitewater issues as the smallest of the others. Perceptive readers might ask themselves "Why?"

Obviously, something the size and scope of "Whitewater" cannot be broken down merely into a series of alphabetized names and items. As a result, this section has been designed to provide amplification on some of the principal parts by reprinting some of these reputable writings that may not have made it to your front porch or mail box.

Appendix A

Whitewater and its various step-sisters

The complex dealings of Whitewater began on Aug. 2, 1978, when Bill Clinton, then Arkansas attorney general, and his wife, Hillary, formed a partnership with James and Susan **McDougal** to purchase 230 acres of land on the White River in northern Arkansas. The couples bought the land for 203,000 dollars—all borrowed—and made plans to develop plots for vacation homes. In September 1979, after Clinton's election as governor of Arkansas, the land was transferred to the new Whitewater Development Corporation, which was co-owned by the two couples. The business was poorly managed, and the Clintons finally sold their interest in the venture to James McDougal in 1992 for 1000 dollars.

The 1989 failure of **Madison** Guaranty, a savings and loan institution run by James McDougal, first drew the attention of government regulators to the Whitewater development. The Resolution Trust Corporation, the federal government agency formed to handle the liquidation of failed savings and loans, issued a report to the Justice Department in late 1992 that detailed possible abuses at Madison Guaranty. The report said that Whitewater had benefited from McDougal's largesse with funds from the savings and loan, and the Clintons were mentioned for their involvement in the Whitewater deal. It cost federal taxpayers 65 million dollars to bail out Madison Guaranty.

Subsequent investigations of the Whitewater affair raised questions about the Clintons' involvement that the administration struggled to put to rest. For example, the president and first lady claimed to have lost almost 69,000 dollars in the failed venture, but there was no documentation that they had ever invested that much, and James **McDougal** asserted that their actual investment was less than 15,000 dollars. Further, the amount of Whitewater-related interest payments that the Clintons deducted from their taxes in the late 1970s and early 1980s was greater than the amount received by the two banks handling their loans. In addition, there were questions about then-Governor Clinton's role in working with **McDougal** in 1986 to pressure David **Hale**, an Arkansas judge and head of a lending company, to grant a 300,000-dollar-loan to Madison Guaranty, more than 100,000 dollars of which ended up in the account of Whitewater. Fuel was added to the controversy when several Clinton Administration officials attempted to impede the investigations by federal bank regulators into the affairs of Madison Guaranty.

—Comptons

The RTC Investigation
The testimony of Jean Lewis

UNITED STATES SENATE
Special Committee to Investigate
Whitewater Development Corporation and Related Matters
Hearings Into the Failure and Resolution of
Madison Guaranty Savings and Loan Association
November 29, 1995
"Mr. Chairman, Distinguished Members of the Committee, my name is Jean Lewis., I was a senior criminal investigator with the Kansas City office of the Resolution Trust Corporation..."

*(**NOTE:** Edited for brevity. In her opening remarks, Ms. Lewis gave*

a summary of her RTC investigation of Madison Guaranty Savings & Loan and the development of referrals sent to the Justice Dept. Ms. Lewis' entire testimony is available from a variety of on-line services and from the federal government).

"Among other things, the referral provided specific check numbers, dates, account names, account balances, particular uses of funds, and the names of individuals and entities involved in various check kiting schemes. The referral also stated that among those who stood to benefit from this activity were Stephen Smith, Jim Guy **Tucker**, then- Governor Bill Clinton and Mrs. Clinton inasmuch as the overdrafts and loan transactions, or alleged check 'swapping' and kiting, between the combined companies' accounts ensured that loan payments and other corporate obligations were met, thus clearly benefiting the principals of each entity.

"Ms. Casey was sworn into office as U.S. Attorney the second week in October 1993. On October 27, 1993, more than a year after its submission, Ms. Casey declined RTC Criminal Referral No. C0004. In other words, Ms. Casey refused to further investigate the matters raised in the referral.

"On November 9, 1993, thirteen days after rejecting the referral, Ms. Casey recused herself from the case. If there was a conflict requiring her to recuse on November 9, 1993, then it would seem there was a conflict when she declined the referral a few days earlier. Nonetheless, rather than investigating further, Ms. Casey rejected the referral stating there was "insufficient information to sustain many of the allegations." But Ms. Casey did have additional information, namely, nine new criminal referrals submitted to her on October 8, 1993. However, Ms. Casey stated she was concurring with the opinion of Justice Department attorneys in Washington who had concluded this matter prior to her coming to the U.S. Attorney's office in Little Rock. But her rejection was in direct conflict with information I had received from the Justice Department in Washington, and the U.S. Attorney's office, when the referral was returned to Little Rock four months earlier.

"As a result of this investigation, nine additional referrals were prepared alleging criminal violations of several sections of the United States Code relating to bank fraud, conspiracy, false statements, false documents, wire fraud, aiding and abetting, and misuse of position.

"These nine referrals identified multiple suspects, including the Bill Clinton Political Committee Fund, James and Susan **McDougal**, Jim Guy **Tucker**, Chris Wade, and several former **Madison** officers and borrowers. As I will discuss later in my testimony, James B. and Susan H. McDougal and Jim Guy Tucker have been indicted and Chris Wade has entered a guilty plea.

"Suspects on some of the referrals overlapped as witnesses on others, reflecting the elaborate nature of Madison's relationships with some of its borrowers. Jim Guy Tucker and former Madison director Charles Peacock III were among those who fell into this category.

"The referrals also identified additional witnesses with potential knowledge of the alleged criminal violations. Those witnesses included Mr. and Mrs. Clinton, Beverly Bassett **Schaffer** and John Selig, of Little Rock's Mitchell Selig Tucker law firm, Stephen Smith, Larry Kuca, and others. Ms. Schaffer and Mr. Selig were law partners of Jim Guy Tucker at Little Rock's Mitchell Selig Tucker law firm. Mr. Selig also acted as general counsel to Madison.

"Ms. Schaffer later was appointed by Governor Clinton to be Arkansas State Securities Commissioner, whose office regulated state savings and loans. These nine referrals, submitted to U.S. Attorney Paula Casey on October 8, 1993, were in her possession and available for her review when she rejected Referral No. C0004 on October 27, 1993

"The Kansas City RTC criminal investigation unit had planned to submit the nine additional criminal referrals on

October 1, 1993. However, RTC Professional Liability Section Chief Julie Yanda obstructed that effort with her unprecedented demand that her staff first conduct a "legal review" of the referrals. Going back to July 1993, shortly after Ms. Yanda was briefed on the criminal referrals, the criminal investigation unit observed the beginning of a concerted effort by the Professional Liability Section (PLS) to monitor the **Madison** investigation and exert control over certain aspects of it.

"At the time, Mr. Curtis had an open line of communication to former Treasury Department General Counsel Jean **Hanson**, who in turn reported to Deputy Treasury Secretary Roger Altman. We now know that Ms. Hanson provided the White House with a "heads up" on the RTC's criminal referrals the day before, on September 29, 1993. We also now know that this "heads up" — which Ms. Hanson has testified she delivered to the White House at Mr. Altman's direction — an assertion that Mr. Altman denies – – resulted in a flurry of activity and communications between the White House and Treasury Department. The request for a legal review of the criminal referrals manipulated standard procedures and provided the Treasury Department the opportunity to review and selectively disseminate sensitive criminal referral information. Such sensitive information was in fact disclosed by Ms. Hanson in her September 29, 1993 visit to the White House."

Beverly Basset Schaffer

—AP wire report, February 25, 1996

Aware of Bill Clinton's friendship with the owner of a failing Arkansas savings and loan, a state regulator warned one of Clinton's aides the federal government was about to crack down, the regulator testified Thursday. Confronted with a handwritten note she sent to the governor's office, Beverly Bassett **Schaffer** said she knew S&L owner James **McDougal** had been a friend of the governor and "I believe ... abused his

139

relationship with Bill Clinton."

Schaffer, the former Arkansas securities commissioner, told the Senate Whitewater Committee that she was concerned McDougal might try to approach the governor's office for help. She said she sent the July 2, 1986, note to aide Sam Bratton so that the governor's office would have nothing further to do with McDougal.

As Schaffer testified, committee Republicans released another note written 12 days after hers, this one by Clinton aide Betsey Wright asking about Clinton's Whitewater real estate venture. Wright's note to Clinton asked whether, in light of McDougal's "current problems," Clinton still had stock in the Whitewater real estate venture. "If so, I'm worried about it," Wright wrote. Clinton scribbled back, "No, don't have any more," with the word "any" underlined. In fact, the Clintons didn't sell their stock in Whitewater until late in 1992, after it had been an issue in the presidential campaign. At the time of Wright's note, McDougal was trying to buy out the Clintons' Whitewater interest and it was unclear who had the company's stock. White House spokesman Mark Fabiani said the president doesn't recall Wright's note.

Republicans, meanwhile, continued their attacks on first lady Hillary Rodham Clinton's veracity, comparing a statement she made under oath to regulators in 1994 with Schaffer's testimony. Schaffer said she informed Mrs. Clinton in a 1985 telephone call that she was comfortable with the idea of issuing stock in McDougal's savings and loan, **Madison** Guaranty. Mrs. Clinton did not mention **Schaffer**'s comment in written answers to federal regulators when questioned about the phone call, saying she had only a vague recollection and was not even certain she made a call to anyone at the state agency. After Schaffer's phone call with Mrs. Clinton, two regulators who worked for Schaffer, Charles Handley and William Brady, raised questions about the plan — which would have involved issuing preferred, non-voting stock in

140

the institution. The proposal was later dropped. Issuing preferred stock had never been done previously by an S&L in Arkansas.

A year later, in 1986, McDougal was about to be removed by federal regulators from the S&L and Schaffer wrote her note to Clinton aide Bratton. She testified that she didn't know at the time that Clinton and McDougal were partners in the Whitewater real estate venture. But she said McDougal had bragged about his relationship with Clinton and she had heard that he tried to exert his influence on the governor's office.

Schaffer's note to the governor's office says, "Madison Guaranty is in pretty serious trouble. Because of Bill's relationship w/McDougal, we probably ought to talk about it." The note says federal regulators would be holding a meeting nine days later — a meeting in which McDougal was removed from control of the S&L. Attached to Schaffer's handwritten note was a three-page letter from federal regulators to Madison Guaranty's board detailing restrictions to be placed on the institution's operations.

Schaffer and committee Democrats said she acted properly in notifying the governor's office. She said there had been press inquiries about the financial condition of Madison Guaranty and she thought the governor's office should know the situation.

"Cattlegate"

—From wire reports

In 1978 and 1979, Hillary Rodham Clinton made about $100,000 in the cattle futures market. This is unusual, as even professional investors tend to lose money in this market. There is speculation that what really happened is that there were two "mirrored" accounts, each of which performed opposite investments.

In this scenario, the paperwork was shuffled afterwards to credit most of the profitable trades to one account and the losses to the other. The mechanism gives the appearance that whoever had the other account was trying to give the Clintons $100,000 under the table. The reason for doing this is that it doesn't look like a bribe or payoff, since both parties appear to have just made some investments. Even without there being a bribe or payoff involved, using mirrored accounts to transfer money is illegal. According to the March 29, 1994 Chicago Tribune, the broker involved in Mrs. Clinton's trades has been sanctioned for using mirrored accounts and other such activities in the same time period as Hillary's profit was made.

On March 29, 1994, the White House released documents summarizing the trades. Mrs. Clinton began with $1,000 in 1978. Her various trades resulted in roughly twice as much profits as losses, for a net gain of $99,537. These trades were made through Ray E. Friedman and Co of Springdale, IL. The account was closed in October 1979. She then opened another account with Stephens, Inc. in Little Rock with $5000, and closed the account in March of 1980 with a small net loss. The documents included monthly summaries of profits and losses, but no detailed trade-by-trade records.

On April 11, 1994, the Clintons revealed that they failed to report $6,498 in income from the commodities trading in 1980, and they paid $14,615 in back taxes and interest. This seems oddly in contrast with the claim that they lost money in their commodities trading account in 1980.

According to the April 1, 1994 USA Today, Mrs. Clinton received "favored treatment" in her trading in that she did not put up the cash normally required to back her investments. At times, "her account was at least $60,000 below the required level."

According to the trade summaries, she made $5300 in a matter of days. Most people who have analyzed the records of the market for that time period have concluded that this was simply not possible with only $1000 invested. According to USA Today, the claim of an initial $5300 profit off her $1000 investment was absolutely impossible. There is also evidence that she didn't pay any trading fees.

One point that has been made is that day trades have lower margin requirements and are easier to adjust (as in record in the "correct" accounts after the profitability is determined) than trades that last overnight. Also, interestingly, it seems from the records that have been released that the profitable trades were the day trades and the losses were from longer term trades.

At first, the White House stated that Mrs. Clinton placed all the trades herself, but now claims that Arkansas lawyer James **Blair** placed orders for most of the trades, despite the fact that the account only allowed Mrs. Clinton to place trades.

Some have suggested that her account may have been mirrored with one owned by Tyson Foods. James **Blair** was also working for Tyson at the same time, which lost three million dollars in the commodities market. Blair sued "Red" **Bone** (Hillary Clinton's broker) in 1983 for misallocating profits and losses among Bone's clients.

The markets she traded in were cattle, soybeans, sugar, hogs, copper, and lumber, though apparently most of the profit was in the cattle futures.

The statute of limitations has expired for this, so it can only be investigated by Congress.

MidLife

*—This article by John Crudelle appeared in the **New York Post** on February 6, 1996*

The Whitewater special prosecutor is looking into whether Hillary Rodham Clinton made other big killings in the commodities market — on top of the time she turned $1,000 into $100, 000.

In addition, probers have recently been asking a lot of questions about wealth and property accumulated by both Bill and Hillary Clinton. And they've been questioning people about campaign gifts to Bill Clinton and unusual stock trading profits by Mrs. Clinton.

Sources who have spoken with the investigators say Whitewater prosecutor Ken Starr seems to be trying to make a case that the Clintons didn't pay some taxes.

The most embarrassing revelation would come if the prosecutor uncovered another instance where Hillary Clinton made a substantial amount of money trading exotic commodities about which she had no expertise.

In 1994, it was revealed that Hillary Clinton turned a $1,000 investment into $100,000 by trading cattle futures. Those transactions occurred in 1978 and 1979. The trades were done with the help of James B. **Blair**, a lawyer for Tyson Foods Inc.

Details about any new trades were sketchy. But a source says investigators are looking into transactions involving other commodities futures contracts, with profits well in excess of what was earned in the cattle market.

Sources also said investigators are asking about other trading activity on the part of Hillary Clinton in stocks through her jointly- owned MidLife investors partnership.

She formed that partnership, in the early 1980s with former Associate Attorney General Webster **Hubbell** (now in prison) and friend Vincent Foster (now dead), whose 1994 death has been the ongoing subject of congressional hearings.

That good fortune in the commodities market was followed in 1980 by a commodities-related venture that netted Mrs. Clinton another $6,498. Mrs. Clinton never reported that profit to the IRS until 1994, when she paid back taxes.

Investigators wouldn't comment. But sources here made it clear that probers are actively on the trail of instances where the Clintons reaped a bounty because of their positions.

One source has been raising serious questions about the amount of possessions that the Clintons took with them from the governor's mansion in Little Rock to the White House.

The source, a Little Rock money manager named Roy Drew, has also told prosecutors of instances where Hillary Clinton, Hubbell and Foster made money trading securities.

"I know they had a lot of home furnishings. I have raised that with everyone I have talked to," says Drew, once the broker for MidLife Investors, the Clinton/Hubbell/Foster investment vehicle. Drew said investigators looking into the Clintons' financial dealings

have contacted him many times. "They are looking at a lot of the financial dealings of the Clintons and related parties," Drew said. Drew recalled some unusual trading in Arkla stock, which rose 40 percent in 45 days because of takeover speculation," Drew said. But Hubbell sold the stock in the company run by another Clinton friend, Thomas McLarty, just days before the Arkla board took measures to prevent a take-over. Drew told investigators that Hubbell made about $3,500 on the $10,000 investment.

Drew also told investigators that Hillary Clinton kept calling to track movement of the Arkla shares — even though Hubbell bought the Arkla stock in his own account, and not in the one he set up with her and Foster. He also told investigators that Hubbell, who was also his neighbor at the time, had told him he was broke right before he deposited $25,000 in the Hutton account.

Other sources have told Starr - and The Post - that Bill Clinton regularly accepted envelopes containing checks and cash, especially during campaign swings. "I told investigators that I picked up envelopes full of cash and checks. One trip I recall, when we went to Denver [in 1988], I picked up probably six or eight envelopes," said Arkansas state trooper Larry **Patterson**.

Patterson said one envelope wasn't sealed, and it contained a $35,000 check to Bill Clinton. That envelope had 15 to 20 other checks in it, along with some cash, Patterson said.

Castle Grande

Castle Grande was an unlikely mix of trailer park, shopping center and brew pub. The 1,000-acre development counted future Gov. Jim Guy Tucker, D-Ark., among its investors. Seth Ward, the father-in-law of Rose Law Firm partner Webb Hubbell, also was involved. Castle Grande was funded by a $1.75 million loan from Madison. The project ultimately cost taxpayers $4 million to clean up.

—This article appeared in **Investors Business Daily** *1996*

Hillary Clinton told the RTC in May 1995 in sworn statements that she knew nothing about Castle Grande. She later explained she knew the transaction only as the Industrial Development Commission, or IDC. But the Rose records cast doubt on the first lady's version. The records include bills from late '85 and '86. They show seven phone calls between Hillary Clinton and Ward from Dec. 6 to Dec. 24. Further contacts occurred in January, February and May of 1986.

In addition, the amount Rose billed suggest that the first lady spent 14.5 hours more on the matter than are reflected in records.

Last week, Ronald Clark, chief executive of Rose, told the Senate Whitewater committee "that is probably exactly what happened." Clark also said that Hillary Clinton had a reputation as "a very meticulous biller."

The IDC defense seems flimsy in light of other records. A Feb. 4, 1986 Rose document mentioned work on a "CG." Clark testified that as the billing partner, Hillary Clinton likely would be familiar with the document.

Another listed IDC and "CG" on the same page. Clark agreed with committee Republicans that CG likely referred to

Castle Grande. A report on Castle Grande prepared for the RTC found that Hillary Clinton probably had some role in the drafting of an option agreement. The report did state there was no proof she did so knowing it was "tied to a straw man contract."

The contract or option in question let Madison purchase land from Ward for $400,000. Investigators believe that deal overvalued the land and served primarily to funnel money to Ward. Ward had been promised commissions on the sale, but bank regulators would likely disapprove of such payments. Indeed, the March 1986 report faulted Madison for paying high commissions to insiders on sales.

Other law firms involved in failed S&L cases found themselves in regulators' cross- hairs. In 1989, Congress told regulators to go after "institution-affiliated" parties.

One California law firm that represented Keating before the state securities board was sued by federal regulators. The firm's connections to then-Gov. George Deukmejian, a Republican, helped to bring it scrutiny. In Arkansas, another law firm paid $12 million to settle claims arising from dealings with a Pine Bluff thrift.

Incredibly, in spite of having worked for Madison, Rose later landed work with the RTC. A suit against Madison's accounting firm brought Rose a $400,000 fee and a $1 million settlement for the RTC.

The RTC report released on Dec. 31 did not have the billing records discovered on Jan. 4 to draw from. But it did find reason to believe some Castle Grande documents were backdated.

Backdating documents is a form of "file stuffing" that was common to failed thrifts. File stuffing at Keating's Lincoln was one of the first signs regulators had of trouble. Questionable land deals like Castle Grande were another common feature of failed thrifts.

"They had an incredible ability to make a mess of things.

They financed ill-conceived projects," Ely said. Criminality usually played a small role. Even when present, most transgressions took place after the institutions were insolvent. In a 1991 study, Ely found that no more than 3% of failures were caused by criminal action.

"A lot of it was just plain incompetence. Some of the things Charlie Keating did were just plain wasteful. David Paul did the same thing in Miami. They built in the wrong place," Ely said.

But when regulators suspected criminality, they went after it with a vengeance. CenTrust Bank Chairman David Paul was sentenced to 11 years and fined $65 million in 1993.

The RTC is still trying to recover assets from him. Earlier this month, Paul was tossed in solitary confinement for possessing unauthorized, civilian underwear. Keating was convicted in 1991 of defrauding investors and sentenced to 10 years.

In August, Starr indicted McDougal and Tucker on fraud charges in connection with loans at Madison. In 1990, McDougal was acquitted of other Madison-related charges.

The RTC's power to investigate the Madison case has been extended to Jan. 31. The agency officially went out of business at the end of last year.

Whitewater Panel on Trail of Hillary Records

—This article appeared as a Reuter wire report February 7, 1996

WASHINGTON (Reuter) - Hillary Rodham Clinton's former law partner Webster **Hubbell** said Wednesday he gave the first lady's legal **billing records** to her friend Vincent Foster in 1992 but did not know who had them when they turned up at the White House last month.

Hubbell said that "I kind of smiled" when the records showing Mrs. Clinton's work for the **Madison** Guaranty savings and loan institution were discovered by a White House aide nearly two years after they had been subpoenaed by federal investigators.

Hubbell said that he and Foster — former partners in the Rose Law Firm in Little Rock, Arkansas — reviewed the bills in early 1992 following press inquiries about the firm's representation of Madison.

The savings and loan is at the center of the tangled Whitewater affair. Its head, James **McDougal**, and his wife were partners with the Clintons in the money-losing vacation development project of that name.

Mrs. Clinton has said her work for **Madison** was minimal, but the records appear to show that she did considerable work on questionable real estate activities by Madison.

Hubbell, **Foster** and the aide who discovered the files, Carolyn **Huber**, came from the Rose firm to Washington with the Clintons. Foster, White House deputy counsel, committed suicide in 1993. Hubbell, who became associate attorney general, is now serving a prison term for defrauding clients.

The Whitewater committee is seeking to find out who left the billing records on a table in a restricted room in the White House residential quarters last August, where they were found by Huber. Huber put them in a box in her own office and did not see them again until January when she realized that they were those being sought by investigators.

The committee is to question White House employees with access to the room at a hearing Thursday.

Hubbell said that after he and Foster and perhaps another Rose lawyer had reviewed the files he gave them to Foster and did not see them again.

He said he did not recall having seen a notation Foster made on the files in red ink, apparently addressed to "HRC."

Asked for his reaction to the discovery of the records, he said, "I kind of smiled." He said he knew **Huber** and was not surprised that it was she who found them.

The committee is trying to trace the custody of the files and Republicans suspect they were removed from Foster's office

149

after his suicide. There has been conflicting testimony on whether papers were taken from his office at a time when authorities were seeking evidence related to his death from a gunshot wound in a park in nearby Virginia.

Other Questioned Clinton Deals

ValuePartners I

—From wire reports

In 1993, when the First Lady was speaking out against the drug industry, a fund that she was investing in sold short on pharmaceutical stocks. The fund apparently profited about $275,000 from the short sales. Mrs. Clinton has stated that the fund was actually long in the stock. This would make sense, if the fund was trying to cover its tracks, but another report claims that the short selling was done by another fund controlled by the one that Mrs. Clinton had directly invested in. This creates the definite appearance of illegal insider trading.

> (**NOTE:** *The Clintons' investments weren't placed into a blind trust until well after this incident.*)

The fund, ValuePartners I, is managed by Smith Capital Management of Little Rock, Arkansas. Mrs. Clinton has been a limited partner since 1986.

The Albany connection

*—This article by Fredric Dicker appeared in the **New York Post**, January 24, 1996*

Neither First Lady Hillary Rodham Clinton nor the Rose Law Firm performed any legal work for the $100,000-plus in fees they got from a New York-funded think tank, it was revealed yesterday.

Attorney General Dennis Vacco, who began probing the payments earlier this month, says the findings "raise a yellow flag, in my mind." Vacco says the contract between the National Center on Education and the Economy and the law firm showed "[Rose] was commissioned as a law firm to implement an educational strategy, and I have to wonder about that." Vacco told Albany radio talk-show host Paul Vandenburg he has written the law firm asking for "billing records, time sheets and the work product" relating to Mrs. Clinton's and the firm's work in 1990 and 1991. He said the firm has not responded. Vacco also said he is seeking a large number of documents and contracts from **NCEE**. He charged that Mrs. Clinton, a member of NCEE's board of directors when the contract was signed in 1990, and Rose, where she was a partner, had "at a very minimum, a cozy relationship" with the organization.

Former Democratic Gov. Mario Cuomo, who served as NCEE's honorary chairman, says he didn't know about the payments to Mrs. Clinton and Rose. Officials at the think tank say she and the law firm were paid to direct its "workforce skills program," but they refuse to provide details. Vacco, a Republican, said NCEE's new law firm - Nixon, Hargrave, Devans and Doyle of Rochester - gave him a copy of the Rose contract and other NCEE-related documents last Friday. The Republican-oriented law firm counts former GOP gubernatorial hopeful Richard Rosenbaum among its partners. Vacco didn't rule out subpoenaing Mrs. Clinton to answer questions about her work for the NCEE. But he insisted: "We're way, way down the line from that." Ron **Clark**, managing partner of the Rose Law Firm in Little Rock, Ark., says he is unaware NCEE made any payments to the First Lady or his firm.

Sources close to Vacco's probe said they believe the money may have been used to underwrite Mrs. Clinton's efforts on behalf of her husband's presidential campaign. Bill Clinton was governor of Arkansas at the time.

Appendix B

Travelgate
The White House Travel Office Scandal

—From wire reports

On January 29, 1993, Darnell **Martens**, businessman and partner (TRM) with Hollywood producer Harry **Thomason** wrote a memo to Thomason suggesting ways Thomason could use his access to the new administration to secure "Washington opportunities" for their aviation consulting firm, TRM. The memo expressed interest in the White House travel office, the charter flight business and a project to review the non-military government aircraft fleet.

Thomason, a personal friend of the Clintons and significant Clinton campaign contributor, told Bill Clinton his company wanted the charter business and could "save the country millions of dollars".

(**NOTE**: *the White House Travel Office did not handle public funds.*)

Rather than exercise the Presidential option to simply fire the at-will employees of the White House Travel Office, Thomason allegedly believed, in the wake of "Nannygate" and other "bad press" for the new administration, it would be an "enhanced press opportunity" to find wrong-doing in the travel office, root it out, fire everyone involved and create positive press by demonstrating a "zero-tolerance" attitude toward corruption and malfeasance while creating the opportunity Thomason and Martens were after.

After further conversations at various times with Bill and Hillary Clinton, Catherine **Cornelius**, Bruce **Lindsey**, William **Kennedy** and Vince Foster, a course of action was decided.

Within a few days of the Thomason-Clinton conversation,

153

Thomason called **Watkins** and told him of the corruption rumors he'd heard. **Watkins** next dispatched Catherine **Cornelius** to work in the travel office for several weeks and report back to him by May 15 on her observations. That is, Cornelius was essentially planted in the office to substantiate rumors that she not only had an interest in fanning but had helped originate in the first place.

Once on the scene, she began eavesdropping on conversations and going through files. She put out the word that some travel office workers were living beyond their means, implying that funds were being embezzled or kicked back from the charter companies. According to sources familiar with the situation, her concerns focused on one employee who owned a cabin on some $10-an-acre property near Virginia's Lake Anna and a $6,000 pontoon boat - hardly high living.

Cornelius also secretly photocopied travel office documents and squirreled them away until she got caught by colleagues one day when a check accidentally jammed the copier and a serviceman had to be called. The travel office people then locked up the files on her, making it impossible for Cornelius to return the papers.

The White House commissioned a "report" from the accounting firm of Peat Marewick to check for accounting errors and irregularities.

But on May 19, 1993, before the Peat Marewick report was issued, David **Watkins** met with the seven staffers of the White House travel office. **Watkins** — the key player in Travelgate, and, strangely, the only one to have been spared press scrutiny — told the startled group, many of whom had served for twenty years, that they were summarily fired. No mention was made of allegations of criminality or of an FBI investigation. Watkins made them surrender their White House passes and ordered them off the premises within an hour.

William H. **Kennedy** III, former Associate White House

Counsel, called in the FBI to "investigate errors and irregularities", intimating the case was of interest "at the highest levels". He allegedly threatened to take his case to the IRS if the FBI couldn't get to it quickly enough.

The head of the travel office, Billy **Dale**, was accused of embezzling $68,000 of reporters' travel money, a charge of which he was later acquitted. Five of the other fired officials were placed in other government jobs and a sixth retired. Catherine **Cornelius** was appointed to run the office. Cornelius had handled travel arrangements for the Clinton Presidential campaign and is the President's second cousin.

A "soul-cleansing" memo by former White House administrator David Watkins turned over to the House Committee on Government Reform and Oversight suggested that Mrs. Clinton was the driving force in the dismissals. Watkins wrote that "there would be hell to pay" if the travel office staff were not fired as the first lady wished.

Later, in a press briefing, McCurry said Clinton insisted that a new General Accounting Office audit showed that improvements have been made in travel office operations.

The audit tells a different story, however. It says that more than two years after **Dale** and his staff were sacked for alleged financial mismanagement, the travel office is rife with accounting problems. The audit found that the travel office rarely follows its own policy of paying airlines and telephone companies within 45 days. It also said employees did not balance the office's books for the first eight months of last year because other tasks were given "a higher priority."

The Travel Office makes about $1.7 million in bookings for White House staff and press travel each year.

As of February 1996...

*—This article by Robert L. Jackson and Robert Ostrow appeared in the **Los Angeles Times** February 13, 1996*

Justice Department attorneys have reportedly shifted their

investigations involving Harry **Thomason** from possible conflict of interests to whether he and a business partner, Darnell **Martens**, impeded the probe. The conflict of interest portion of the inquiry had focused on whether Thomason used a White House office and credentials early in the Clinton administration to lobby for an aviation firm he co-owned to be bought in to take over the White House Travel Office. That area of the probe ended with the determination that Thomason's White House ties did not make him a federal employee subject to the governments conflict-of interest laws.

Officials have not closed the criminal investigation, however. They are reviewing whether their inquiry was impeded by erroneous information given to them by Martens, Thomason's partner in the aviation consulting firm TRM. A House committee portrayed Thomason as the source of early White House rumors that employees in the travel office, headed by Billy R. Dale were "on the take" from transpiration firms that handled travel by the White House press corps. The FBI found no evidence to support the rumors.

White House memos and testimony before the House Government Reform and Oversight Committee show that Thomason urged the firings in direct conversations with the Clintons and with then-presidential aides David **Watkins**, William **Kennedy** and the late Vincent **Foster**.

For **Thomason** to be charged with conflict-of-interest violations, he would have to have been either a full-time federal official or a "special government employee." The General Accounting Office, the investigative arm of Congress, concluded that he did not fit into either category. The GAO's finding was based on the fact that **Thomason** received no government pay, did not have a permanent White House office and his White House pass was only temporary. The Justice Department reportedly has reached the same conclusion.

Appendix C

The Death of Vince Foster

On July 20, 1993, the body of Deputy White House Counsel **Vincent Foster** was found in **Fort Marcy Park** near Washington D.C., only hours after the FBI had raided the Little Rock offices of David **Hale**. His death was ruled a suicide.

Subsequently, a furor was raised over the disposition of papers in Foster's office, and strong charges were lodged that the White House directed and covered up an attempt to remove and sterilize those files. The files in question are believed by some to be related to Whitewater, while some others suspect they are related to national security issues involving **Mena** and alleged money laundering. In addition, the characterization of Foster's death itself has been called into question, with some respected forensic experts and material witnesses contradicting important aspects of the official version.

The autopsy

Vince Foster's autopsy was conducted by the deputy medical examiner for Northern Virginia, **Dr. James Beyer**. Beyer, 77, has conducted thousands of autopsies in his career, but in recent years has come under some criticism in rulings on suicide cases, including the following:

The New York Post and The Washington Times reported that **Beyer** had ruled incorrectly in the case of 21-year-old Timothy Easley, who Beyer said died of a self-inflicted stab wound. Easley's girlfriend later confessed to Easley's murder, but only after the family had another pathologist, Dr. Harry Bonnell, deputy chief medical examiner of San Diego, review photos they had taken of cuts to Easley's hand, "The cut on the hand is definitely ante mortem, and I cannot understand how any competent forensic pathologist would miss it. It is a classical defense wound, suffered while trying to avoid the knife," Bonnell concluded

In another case — the 1991 death of 21 year-old Tommy Burkett — **Beyer** ruled Burkett's death consistent with a self-inflicted gunshot. Burkett's alleged suicide was similar to Foster's — apparent death by a revolver fired in the mouth. The Burkett family undertook a second autopsy and found that Beyer had failed to note that Burkett had trauma to his ear and abrasions to his chest, indications he may have been beaten first. Beyer also claimed to have dissected Burkett's lungs, but a second autopsy showed that procedure had never been done.

Several issues relating to **Beyer's** autopsy of Foster remain:

Missing x-rays: **Beyer's** autopsy report indicates X-rays were taken of Foster. But Beyer now says his X-ray machine was "inoperable." The police report quotes Beyer as stating "that X-rays indicated that there was no evidence of bullet fragments in the head." X-rays would help substantiate the written autopsy report.

Exit wound: Fairfax County emergency medical technician Kory Ashford told the FBI last year that while he placed Foster's body in a body bag by grasping his shoulders and cradling his head, he did not see any exit wound — though the autopsy report said the bullet exited the top of the back of the head. Ashford said he saw little or no blood, didn't need gloves, and didn't wash his hands after the task.

Fiske claimed in his report that Foster had a large exit wound, yet the medical examiner on the scene told the FBI the wound was consistent with a low-velocity weapon. Foster was found with a high velocity .38-caliber revolver. The lead police investigator said the wound was small.

Trauma or sign of struggle: Critical to any determination of suicide is a careful examination for additional wounds to the body, needle marks or other signs of a struggle, Beyer noted no such signs. But a Polaroid picture taken at the scene and enhanced during Starr's inquiry before the grand jury earlier this year, showed what "appeared to be a wound, puncture or other trauma" to the right side of Foster's neck near to the jaw line, a source said. The photo, which was apparently never enhanced for review by **Fiske**'s expert panel, finds some eerie corroboration in the statement made by emergency medical technician **Richard Arthur** who told the FBI last year "he noted what appeared to be a small caliber bullet hole in Foster's neck on the right side, just under the jaw line about halfway between the ear and the tip of the chin."

Drugs, alcohol analysis: Blood lab work attached to Beyer's report indicates no drugs or alcohol were detected in Foster's blood. Later the FBI analyzed the blood sample and reported to **Fiske** that it found trace amounts of an anti-depressant and Valium in Foster's blood, though Beyer's lab had tested for these very drugs.

The suicide note

James **Davidson**, publisher and editor of the *Strategic Investment* newsletter, commissioned a panel of three international handwriting experts to examine the Foster suicide note. In a triple blind test (i.e., each independent of the other) all concluded it was a forgery. Information about the lack of proper FBI analysis of the note was highlighted in their disclosure at a press conference lightly covered by the mainstream media.

The three experts were:

Mr. Reginald E. Alton, from Oxford University, was flown in for this conference. He is a world-recognized expert on handwriting and manuscript authentication. For 30 years he has lectured at Oxford on handwriting, and has engaged in forensic document examination. Recently he ruled on the authenticity of C.S. Lewis's Diaries. He has been consulted by British police authorities and has testified in British courts on both criminal and civil matters involving questioned documents.

Mr. Vincent Scalice, is formerly a homicide expert with the New York City Police Department. He is a certified Questioned Document Examiner with the American Board of Forensic Examiners. He has 22 years experience as a document examiner, and has worked for some of the country's largest institutions in this capacity, for example Citicorp and Chemical Bank.

Mr. Ronald Rice has 18 years experience performing civil, criminal and forensic handwriting examination. He is a consultant to the Massachusetts Attorney General's office. He has examined documents on a number of celebrated cases, and was asked by CNN to examine notes written by O.J. Simpson during coverage of the Simpson trial.

A synopsis of their findings:

—From an editorial by Deroy Murdock, President, **Loud & Clear Communications**

"The forger," Alton said by phone, "was probably using bits and pieces of Foster's documents, but he doesn't understand the way Foster writes." This is evident even to the untrained eye. Foster used the cursive form of the letter "I" when referring to himself in his known documents. In the suicide note, the letter "I" stands capitalized, as stiff as a steel beam. The letters "Th," are joined together with a loop over the "h." In the suicide note, they appear repeatedly as two separate, distinct elements.

There are subtler anomalies as well.

"Foster's hand is fluid, fluent and highly cursive," Alton

said. "Where possible he'll make a complicated letter in one stroke rather than two or three. The so-called suicide note, in fact, makes 'b' in three quite deliberate strokes." Added Alton, "The spaces are not the same. The slope is uncertain."

Handwriting aside, the note's contents don't signal suicide.

"It makes no mention of intentional harm to one's self," Scalice observed in his written report.

"Significantly, there is no mention of characteristic statements of departure for loved ones, the putting of affairs in order, or a motive for suicide."

Instead, the note is primarily a list of Foster's complaints about his professional life.

It concludes: "I was not meant for the job or the spotlight of public life in Washington. Here ruining people is considered sport."

While it suggests that Foster was overwhelmed and perhaps despondent about his duties, nothing approximates the "Goodbye, cruel world" tone one would expect from someone on the verge of gunning himself down.

Two days after Foster's death, then White House Counsel Bernard Nussbaum (who later resigned under an ethical cloud) searched Foster's briefcase and reportedly declared, "It's empty."

Four days later, the suicide note was found inside the same satchel, torn into 27 pieces. The 28th piece still is missing from the unsigned, undated, fingerprint-free note.

"If you tear a note, it obscures all of the characteristics that are in the normal handwriting: the way one letter is joined to another, the way words run along a line, the way margins are registered," Alton said. "This is enough to make one suspicious."

U.S. Park Police and one-time Whitewater Special Prosecutor Robert **Fiske** both concluded that Foster wrote the note. But they rendered their verdict after rather cursory investigations.

The Park Police called on U.S. Capitol Police Sgt. Larry Lockhart to examine the note.

Lockhart, who is not a board-certified handwriting analyst, compared the note with just one other sample of Foster's writing.

Federal guidelines require scrutinizing a dubious document against at least four known writing samples. **Fiske** relied on the FBI, which examined a one-page document and two checks Foster wrote.

According to an Oct. 25 Pittsburgh Tribune-Review article by reporter Christopher Ruddy, the FBI lab found Foster's checks and the suicide note to be an "inconclusive match."

The witnesses

—From wire reports

Pat Knowlton

Pat Knowlton, a construction consultant, stopped at Ft. Marcy park the afternoon of July 20, 1993 for the inglorious purpose of taking a leak in the bushes. As he parked his car, he saw that there were two other cars in the park — a brown Honda, later identified as Vince Foster's car, and a blue sedan. It was this second car, or rather its occupant, that caught Knowlton's attention. The young man, later described by Knowlton as an Hispanic man in his twenties with a thin face, gave him a "menacing" look. Knowlton was sufficiently unnerved by the stare that he left his wallet in his car as he went about his urgent business, fearing an assault.

As **Knowlton** quickly relieved himself by a nearby tree, the Hispanic man got out of his blue sedan and stood leaning over the roof of the car. Frightened, Knowlton said he quickly left the park, but mentally noted some of the contents of the Arkansas Honda, including a suit jacket and a briefcase.

162

Knowlton called the park police later the same night after he heard on the news of Foster's death. The police took a brief statement from him over the phone, which they included in their report but spelled his name wrong. According to the report, no briefcase was found in Foster's car. Foster's brief-case later turned up at the White House.

Further, Knowlton has angrily denounced a key statement attributed to him by the FBI during the **Fiske** investigation as "an outright lie." The FBI agents who interviewed him wrote, "Knowlton could not further identify this individual (the Hispanic man) and stated that he would be unable to recognize him in the future." In fact, Knowlton was able to provide a police artist with a description which was rendered as a sketch.

He has thus far not been called by the Starr investigators.

Thomas Castleton

*—This article by Christopher Ruddy appeared in the **Pittsburgh Tribune-Review** February 6, 1996*

A White House staffer, among the last people to see Vincent Foster alive, has told federal investigators that Foster was carrying a briefcase when he left his office on the day of his death.

> *(**NOTE**: This account directly contradicts two federal investigations that have painted a scenario of Foster leaving his office without his briefcase.)*

In 1994, Thomas **Castleton**, a young staffer in the White House Counsel's Office - where Foster was a deputy - told investigators for Special Counsel Robert **Fiske** that when he saw Foster leave his West Wing office, Foster was holding a briefcase, according to a source familiar with **Fiske**'s probe.

Several witnesses who say they saw Foster's car in **Fort Marcy Park** on July 20, 1993 - before and after police arrived to investigate the discovery of Foster's body - also have apparently told **Fiske**'s investigators they saw what appeared to be a briefcase or attaché case on the seat of Foster's Honda.

163

Castleton's testimony adds further weight to their observations. It also further fuels speculation that - as some investigators believe - a cover-up of the death may have been under way early on the night of the death and that the removal of the briefcase from the crime scene at Fort Marcy may have been part of that effort.

Official Park Police investigative and evidence reports make no mention of a briefcase, and several policemen have testified pointedly under oath that there was no briefcase at the scene, according to sources. Castleton, since promoted to the Department of Justice's Office of Legislative Affairs, declined to comment on the matter for the Tribune-Review.

Despite the possible implications of Castleton's account, **Fiske**, in his June 1994 report on Foster's death, made no mention of Castleton's recollection of seeing Foster leave with the briefcase. Instead, he offered another account.

The Senate Banking Committee signed off on **Fiske**'s report after a single day of hearings in July 1994. The committee also released more than 2,500 pages of documents and FBI interview statements given to it for review by **Fiske**'s staff. Castleton's interview statement was not included in those documents, which have been made public.

Castleton's interview statement, however, was included in material **Fiske** turned over to his successor. **Fiske**, the original Whitewater special prosecutor, was later replaced by Kenneth Starr.

According to the **Fiske** report, Foster left work on the day of his death at about 1 p.m. after eating lunch in his office. Soon after that, he drove to suburban Washington's **Fort Marcy Park**, where he shot himself in the head with a 1913 Colt .38 caliber revolver.

The report addresses the issue of a briefcase. On Page 26 is the following: "At about 1 p.m., (Foster) came out of his office holding his suit jacket, without a briefcase. He told (Linda) Tripp (the top assistant) that there were still some M&M's on the tray if she wanted them. He said, `I'll be back,' and then left."

Foster never did return, leaving major questions in his wake for investigators: Where was Foster going? Why did it take so long for his body to be found (nearly five hours)? Why didn't anyone see him in the interim?

Two prosecutors told the Tribune-Review that if Castleton's statement about the briefcase had been accepted by **Fiske**'s investigators, it would have raised the possibility of a cover-up (the improper removal of the briefcase from the crime scene) and of foul play in the death (where was Foster before he was found in the park?).

The only statement by Castleton in the material given to the Senate Banking panel is a brief one found in the Park Police report compiled shortly after Foster's death. Castleton told the Park Police that he "was present when Mr. Foster left the office after eating lunch and said `So long.' Mr. Foster did not respond and seemed to Mr. Castleton to be `in his own world,' focused and disturbed."

The written account of the Park Police interview with Castleton on July 22, 1993, makes no mention of any briefcase. Yet the briefcase becomes an issue in the police interview that immediately followed Castleton's, the interview of Linda Tripp, executive assistant to

White House Counsel Bernard Nussbaum. The police account of Tripp's interview has her "absolutely certain that Mr. Foster did not carry anything in the way of a briefcase, bag, umbrella, etc. ... out of the office."

The issue of the briefcase cropped up early last year during grand jury proceedings in Washington led by Associate Independent Counsel Miguel Rodriguez. Rodriguez eventually resigned from Starr's staff to return to his post as an assistant U.S. attorney in Sacramento, Calif. The Tribune-Review has reported that Rodriguez' superiors had thwarted his efforts to conduct a full probe. The stunted grand jury proceedings brought no indictments.

But two sources close to Starr's probe confirmed for the Tribune-Review that at one point their investigation had focused on the possibility that someone had returned the briefcase to the White House. The matter was not pursued after Rodriguez left.

During grand jury testimony, a ranking Park Police officer said that a "liaison officer" with the Secret Service was present at Fort Marcy on the night of the death. The presence of an additional law enforcement agent contradicts official records, the sworn testimony of some officers, and claims that the death investigation was solely handled by the Park Police.

During grand jury proceedings last year, at least four park policemen testified there was no briefcase at the scene. However, Rodriguez had turned up photographic evidence of a black briefcase lying in the vicinity of Foster's car. The police said it was a carrying case for crime scene equipment, but during proceedings admitted that their cases are tan or silver, not black like the one depicted in an enhanced photograph.

Testimony also demonstrated that the briefcase found at Fort Marcy was not the leather satchel found in Foster's office after his death, and one in which a torn note surfaced almost a week later. Foster was said to rarely, if ever, have carried that case.

Patrick **Knowlton**, the first known witness to have spotted Foster's Honda in Fort Marcy's lot, told **Fiske**'s FBI agents that he "observed in this Honda a leather briefcase or leather folder on the passenger side seat."

Similarly, at least two emergency workers told **Fiske**'s investigators and Starr's grand jury they saw a briefcase after the police arrived. Paramedic Sgt. George **Gonzalez** told the FBI, "The Honda contained a necktie, suit coat, and a black briefcase/ attaché case."

Shortly after Rodriguez' departure, Starr effectively closed down the investigation into Foster's death, and no indictments have been handed up.

The make-up artist

*—This article by Christopher Ruddy appeared in the **Pittsburgh Tribune-Review** February 13 1996*

WASHINGTON - It is said to be one of the closely guarded secrets involving the federal probes into the death of Vincent Foster. And for good reason: it indicates to some investigators not only that a cover-up was underway early on the night of Foster's death, but also that President Clinton may have been linked to those activities.

The secret: A make-up artist for CNN's Larry King Live program has told federal investigators that she overheard a conversation indicating Clinton was aware of Foster's death before he appeared on the King show live from the White House library. According to a source, the make-up artist came forward in 1994 to tell her story during the latter part of Special Counsel Robert **Fiske**'s investigation into Foster's death. The woman told investigators that as she was applying make-up to Clinton's face at the White House - shortly before the program's 9 p.m. air time - an unidentified male presumed to be an aide notified Clinton that a note had been found in Foster's office.

The president and White House officials say that he was not notified of the death until about 10 p.m., over an hour later, by Chief of Staff Mack McLarty.

White House officials also say that no officials entered Foster's office until about 10 p.m. and that no notes or documents relating to the attorney's death were found or removed from the office that evening. The young make-up artist has told investigators that McLarty was present when the president was informed about activities in Foster's office. She was unable to identify the man who spoke with the president. Her account was taken seriously enough that investigators had her review photos of White House staffers. She was still unable to identify the person, the source said.

The make-up artist, who has left CNN to work in CNBC's Washington Bureau, told the Tribune-Review she could not comment on the matter. "I usually don't discuss my clients and what goes on. It's not a good practice," she said.

Fiske issued his Foster report June 30, 1994, concluding that there was no evidence of foul play or a cover-up of the death. The make-up artist's account was not mentioned. A month later, two of **Fiske**'s FBI investigators stated those conclusions for a Senate Banking Committee hearing. In neither instance did the make-up artist's account surface.

Sources close to the Senate committee probe of the death said they were not informed of the woman's claims by **Fiske**, or provided with her FBI statement. **Fiske** released dozens of FBI statements to the committee, which have since been made public. The make-up artist's statement was not included in those released. Her statement was considered credible by investigators because of other evidence that the White House knew earlier about the death than it claimed.

Her comments are also consistent with information gathered by investigators that an intruder alarm went off in the White House counsel's office, which includes Foster's, just after 7 p.m. on the night of his death - but well before the time the White House claimed it was notified by Park Police that Foster was dead. An alarm again went off after 10 p.m., but officials claim to have been notified by then.

OFFICIAL VERSION

During a press conference the day after Foster's death, conducted by Communications Director Mark **Gearan** and McLarty, Gearan laid out the official White House chronology of events. During that time, Gearan had a testy exchange with reporters, who were incredulous about the statement that it took nearly four hours to confirm Foster was dead. Foster's body was found by Park Police just after 6 p.m. Police say a single gunshot wound to his head was self-inflicted.

Gearan said that White House security aide, Craig

168

Livingstone, a political appointee of the Clintons, was notified at about 8:30 p.m. of the Foster matter, and that the White House's chief administrative officer, David **Watkins**, was notified about 9 p.m. "Soon after the (Larry King) show began, we were pulled from the staff room where ... McLarty was informed of this - that it was an unconfirmed report," Gearan said. "In the intervening 50 or so minutes, efforts were made to both confirm and to make preliminary calls. ..."

Confirmation, Gearan said, came at 9:55 p.m., and only then was Clinton told. The president was finishing his first hour with King when McLarty informed him of a problem, and Clinton had to renege on his offer to King to continue for an additional half-hour. According to Newsweek, Clinton asked McLarty, "What is it? It's not Hillary or Chelsea." The two went up to the residence quarters of the White House where Clinton was told of Foster's death. "Oh no," the president reportedly cried out. Calls to the White House and **Fiske** for comment on this story went unreturned.

The Tribune-Review has reported that investigators for Kenneth Starr, **Fiske**'s successor, have said that at one point they were examining the possibility that White House officials knew about the death much earlier. Some investigators believed that the time of the official notification to the White House may have been extended to allow for unnamed officials to engage in an examination of Foster's office and possibly the crime scene before any law enforcement authorities, such as the FBI, could assert jurisdiction and secure the scene and premises.

Several points of evidence and testimony suggest that the long delay in notification of the death doesn't jibe with the facts. These include:

Grand jury evidence turned up last year that members of the Special Forces, an elite unit of the Park Police closely associated with White House Security, were at **Fort Marcy Park** - where Foster's body was found - by 7 p.m. on the night of death.

Several accounts by police and emergency workers that demonstrate officials knew Foster was a White House official by 7 p.m. after searching his car early in the evening and finding his White House identification card. These accounts directly contradict the testimony of other Park Police that they stumbled upon the ID after entering the car much later, at about 8:30 p.m.

The sworn statements of two Arkansas State troopers that Chelsea Clinton's nanny, Helen Dickey, called the Arkansas governor's mansion earlier on the evening of the 20th - as early as 6 p.m. Washington time - to notify Gov. Guy **Tucker** of the death. Officials say that Foster's body was not even found until after 6 p.m.

Additionally, London's Sunday Telegraph reported a Secret Service log shows that just after 7 p.m., security officials cleared a "MIG" Group - a military intelligence group - into the White House West Wing. They met with presidential assistant Patsy Thomasson. Thomasson admitted to entering Foster's office later that night. The Secret Service told the Telegraph the MIG group's activities are classified.

"MIG" — a peculiar twist

*—This article by Ambrose Evans-Pritchard appeared in **The London Daily Telegraph**, January 27, 1996*

Now it has emerged that logs kept by Secret Service staff at the White House — published in Senate documents on the death of Mr. Foster — show that a so-called "MIG Group" was checked into offices occupied by Miss **Thomasson** and her boss, David **Watkins** — on the ground floor of the West Wing — at 7.10pm on July 20, 1993.

Miss Thomasson was the only member of the White House staff logged into the office at the time. She checked out at the same time as the "MIG Group" at 7.44 PM, after sharing the office with them for 34 minutes (confusingly, her name is misspelt several times in the logs).

The White House has failed to explain why this "MIG Group" appeared in the logs. Miss Thomasson herself slammed down the telephone before I had finished asking a question.

The press spokesman for the Secret Service at first said that he had not heard of the acronym "MIG".

The next day he changed his account, saying that the "MIG Group" was a team of Secret Service technicians that had gone to Miss Thomasson's office that night to conduct a routine alarm check. He said he could not divulge what the acronym MIG stood for because the unit was secret.

But there is no other mention of this "MIG Group" in logs of other offices covering a two-week period in July 1993, which suggests that the visit to Miss Thomasson's office was not routine.

There is another explanation. Intelligence sources have told The Sunday Telegraph that "MIG" stands for "military intelligence group". MIG groups are typically known as Technical Services Counter-Measure teams (TSCMs), highly classified units that handle high-tech counter-espionage. Their duties, for example, include sweeping for bugs at the White House.

Sources say that the high-tech counter-espionage staff at the White House are controlled and operated by the Federal Emergency Management Agency, known as FEMA. This agency, often singled out by the anti-government militia movement as the biggest single threat to liberty in America, has enormous power and can draw freely on the capabilities of the CIA, the FBI, and the Pentagon.

Miss Thomasson has admitted entering Foster's White House office on the night of his death. She testified to the Senate Whitewater Committee that she went in to look for a suicide note - she said the door was open - but she denies removing any documents.

But the visit to the Foster office about which she testified took place at around 11pm. The newly-discovered Secret Service logs raise the possibility that there was some sort of "damage control" meeting going on with intelligence technicians much earlier, at 7.10pm.

In themselves, the logs prove nothing. But they add to the growing weight of evidence that a tiny group at the White House was tipped off early about Foster's death, long before the official notification at 8.30pm. It would have provided a window of at least an hour to cover things up before anybody was alerted.

If so, America is facing a White House scandal that is every bit as serious and nasty as Watergate.

Appendix D

The Conspiracy Morass

"Fostergate" (August 1995, Media Bypass)

"Fostergate" alleges that Vince Foster was a behind-the-scenes overseer on behalf of the NSA for the Arkansas company **Systematics** Inc., founded by Jackson Stephens. Systematics was selling the bank processing software PROMIS designed by the small Washington DC company **Inslaw**.

After Forbes spiked the Fostergate story, Norman sent Forbes editor James W. Michaels a memo urging him to reconsider. But the memo made another allegation that Norman attributed to anonymous CIA sources: that Caspar Weinberger, a former Defense Secretary and now Forbes' chairman, was one of "scores" of government officials who had stashed millions in Swiss accounts. Norman claimed that the booty had been wiped out by a renegade band of CIA computer hackers, the "Fifth Column". The embarrassing memo was particularly ill timed. Malcolm S. "Steve" Forbes Jr., 48-year-old Forbes editor-in-chief, was readying a campaign to run for President. Only hours after receiving the memo, Norman says, Michaels gave him a choice: to take indefinite unpaid leave or accept a severance package. Norman resigned, and has thus sided with "conspiracists" who believe that Foster was murdered to cover up an immense national and international scandal.

The part of his report about CIA "5th column hackers", a

small band of principled CIA (and possibly FBI, DEA and/or IRS agents) who have broken into foreign intelligence computers and transferred billions of dollars without detection has given Norman some "credibility" problems in certain quarters. However, many other aspects correlate highly with the findings of other sources.

Transcribed from a 1995 radio interview:

Jim Norman:

["Fostergate"] was originally written for Forbes Magazine, where until 8/18/95 I was a senior editor. For reasons officially unknown to me, but, I believe, unrelated to legitimate editorial concerns, Forbes chose not to run the story despite its passing the usual rigorous fact-checking process at Forbes and libel review by Forbes' outside counsel. Forbes Editor James Michaels gave me permission to publish the story elsewhere so long as I did not identify myself as working for Forbes. Subsequent to the killing of the story by Forbes, a senior publishing executive with the magazine confided to me privately that the reason the story died had something to do with Caspar Weinberger, former Sec. of Defense and now Forbes publisher.

Systematics (now Alltel Information Services) has tried diligently to suppress this story. Aside from the pressure brought on Forbes (which gets about $1 million a year in advertising from parent Alltel Corp.), their libel attorney Charles O. Morgan has sent threatening letters all over the place trying to preempt other publications from running it or even discussing it on the radio. A serious consideration of these threats would show they are hollow. But the media is a business. Publishers shy away from lawsuits, even if they can be won.

Paul Rodriguez, the editor of Washington-based Insight magazine, has told me he received a visit from a military intelligence guy from the Pentagon who told him bluntly to "Lay off this story. You don't know what you're dealing with."

Anthony Kimery, a fellow journalist who has corroborated much of this story from his own intelligence sources, was summarily fired as editor of a Thomson financial publication, apparently because he was asking too many questions about PROMIS (which a Thomson unit in Canada may have been involved in selling or modifying). Sarah McClendon had her newsletter dropped from an AT&T controlled electronic news service because she pursued the **Systematics** connection. And, of course, I have now been fired from Forbes for, I believe, asking too many questions about Cap Weinberger's Swiss bank accounts and possibly even causing one of them to be raided for $2.3 million in illicit funds.

On top of that, even the investigators for Rep. James Leach's House Banking Committee seem to be aiding and abetting the cover-up by tipping Morgan off as soon as they learned Media Bypass was going to publish the story, and then going out of their way to impugn and intimidate my sources, even trying to lure one of them into committing a felony by hacking into a bank database. I now have an exceedingly low regard for Mr. Leach and his staff.

Mena

A subject tirelessly discussed on the Internet, but sparsely in mainstream discourse, Mena refers collectively to the apparently intertwined activities centering around the Intermountain Airport in Mena, Arkansas. Some of these activities involved several associates of Bill Clinton, who was governor of Arkansas during the tenure of Iran-contra.

Barry Seal

(**NOTE**: *As an established radio/TV personality in Baton Rouge back in the early 1970's, I had the dubious distinction of calling Barry Seal a client. Along with my morning radio show, I ran my own advertising agency. Among other interests, Barry was trying to grow his small portable sign business; he hired my firm to advertise and promote it. While I will not detail here what all of my duties and services eventually entailed, suffice to say Barry wasn't someone who thought small—or trusted many.—BW)*

—From the **Arkansas Gazette**

After becoming one of the youngest pilots in the history of Trans-World Airlines at 26, Seal turned to smuggling in 1972. He was arrested on his first trip, a shipment of plastic explosives to anti-Castro Cubans in Mexico. The charges were dropped, and Seal switched to hauling marijuana and then cocaine.

(Arkansas State Police investigator Russell) Welch has said that investigators who began looking into Seal's operation in the early 1980s found indications that he was smuggling cocaine into Mena basically the same way he smuggled it into Louisiana. One indication was the presence of helicopters at the airport. Seal's *modus operandi* when he was based in Louisiana was to drop the contraband by parachute into remote, swampy areas, where his operatives would pick it up by helicopter and take it for further distribution by automobile.

Seal became an informant for the federal Drug Enforcement Agency in March 1984 after being convicted earlier that year in Fort Lauderdale, Fla., of smuggling methaqualone into the country. As an informant, Seal helped the DEA make several important cases. In the most celebrated case, he operated hidden cameras mounted by the CIA inside one of his cargo planes and captured photos of Medellin cartel leaders and Nicaraguan government officials loading drugs onto the plane on an airstrip in Nicaragua. That plane later ended up being used in the secret effort organized by Lt. Col. Oliver North to resupply the Contra rebels in Nicaragua. It was shot down Oct. 5, 1986, over Nicaragua, with Eugene Hasenfus the sole survivor. The plane's co-pilot, Buzz Sawyer of Magnolia, Ark., was killed in the crash. The plane's connection with Seal is viewed as corroborating evidence by those who claim that the Contra supply network was financed with drug-smuggling profits from the U.S.

The state police file indicates that investigators in Arkansas and Louisiana suspected Seal was using his DEA cover to run his own smuggling missions on the side. The connections between the federal government and Barry Seal went deeper than just the DEA, according to a one-time associate of the smuggler.

Terry Reed

—From wire reports

Terry Reed, a former Little Rock businessman and pilot, has said that in 1983 he met Barry Seal through Oliver North, who organized the secret Contra resupply effort. Reed said Seal later recruited him to train Latin American pilots at a grass airstrip operated by Seal at Nella in rural Scott County. Reed's revelations about Seal emerged as a result of federal charges filed against Reed. The mail fraud charges stemmed from his own connections to North, whom he said he met in Thailand during the Vietnam War.

Reed has maintained that Oliver North had asked him to "donate" his plane to the Contra effort in 1983 by allowing it to be stolen, pocketing the insurance on it and then "forgetting" about it. Reed claimed he refused but that his plane was stolen anyway and he did claim insurance on it. The plane later turned up back in Reed's garage, and he was charged with fraud.

Some, including federal prosecutors who charged Reed, dismissed Reed's tale as fabrication.

But it was never put to a test. When Reed's trial was scheduled to start, prosecutors agreed to acquittal if, Reed said, he would remain quiet for at least 30 days. "They told me they didn't want me having a press conference," Reed said.

Kevin Ives and Don Henry

—From wire reports

Kevin **Ives** and Don **Henry**, were two Bryant, Arkansas teenage boys whose bodies were found August 23, 1987 lying side by side on railroad tracks near the Mena airport. Ives had a fractured skull and the bottom parts of both their legs were amputated. The Arkansas State medical examiner, Dr. Fahmy Malak (appointed by then-Governor Clinton), ruled the boys had "fallen asleep" on the railroad tracks where their bodies were found, arms neatly at their sides. The medical examiner continued, "Apparently the boys didn't hear the train coming; they were stoned out of their minds on pot." Ives' mother, Linda, won the legal right to have the bodies exhumed and reautopsied by an independent medical examiner who found the cause of death was murder by beating and stabbing before they were placed on the railroad tracks.

Other mysterious deaths around Mena

Six local people came forward independently, each claiming to have some special knowledge about the deaths of the boys on the track. All six were killed prior to testifying.

Keith Koney

Died in a motorcycle accident in July 1988 with unconfirmed reports of a high speed car chase.

Keith McKaskle

He was stabbed to death in November 1988.

Gregory Collins

He died from a gunshot wound to the face in January 1989.

Jeff Rhodes

Claimed to have information on the deaths of **Ives**, **Henry** & McKaskle. His burned body was found in a trash dump in April 1989. He died of a gunshot wound to the head and there was some body mutilation, leading to the speculation that he was probably tortured prior to being killed.

James Milam

Claimed to have had information on the **Ives** & **Henry** deaths. He was decapitated. The state Medical examiner, Fahmy Malak, initially ruled death due to natural causes.

Richard Winters

Winters was a suspect in the deaths of Iv**es** & **Henry**. He was killed in a "robbery" in July 1989 which was subsequently proven to be a setup.

Jordan Kettleson

Claimed to have had information on the **Ives** & **Henry** deaths. He was found shot to death in the front seat of his pickup in June 1990.

Inslaw and the Systematics connection

—From wire reports and other sources

Inslaw is a small computer company owned by William and Nancy Hamilton.

Inslaw markets case management software to courts and related justice agencies, to the insurance industry, to large law firms, and to the law departments of corporations. Inslaw's principal asset is a highly sophisticated software program called PROMIS, a computer program which manages large amounts of information.

In 1982, Inslaw signed a $10 million contract with the Justice Department to install their PROMIS software into offices of forty-two U.S. Attorneys. The person assigned by the Department to manage the contract, however, was one C. Madison Brewer, who had just been fired by Inslaw. Just one month after the contract was signed, Mr. Brewer recommended that it be terminated even though Inslaw was performing as agreed.

Incurring heavy debt, Inslaw obtained a loan to complete the contract, but upon installation the Justice Department refused to pay, thus forcing them into bankruptcy.

(Note: Close friend of then-Attorney General Edwin Meese, Earl Brian, had a controlling interest in a competing computer company called Hadron, Incorporated.)

180

Brian allegedly was linked to covert operations with the United States and Israeli intelligence communities and reportedly worked for the CIA. Previously, Hadron's chairman had attempted to purchase the PROMIS software from Inslaw but they had refused to sell. After Inslaw sought refuge in Chapter 11, pressure from the IRS forced Inslaw into Chapter 7 liquidation which would open the door for Hadron to acquire the PROMIS software. The Hamiltons and their attorney, former U.S. Attorney General Elliot Richardson, filed a civil suit claiming the Justice Department appropriated PROMIS to give the software to Earl Brian to raise money for covert actions and to turn it over to the National Security Agency for marketing to foreign intelligence services. While PROMIS software was designed to keep track of law enforcement cases, it could also be used to keep tabs on political dissidents, mass movement via wire transfer or deposits of large amounts of cash typical of money laundering.

U.S. Bankruptcy Judge George Bason, who ruled in favor of Inslaw in the civil trial, awarded the Hamiltons $6.8 million and found, in September 1987, that Justice Department officials "took, converted and stole" PROMIS through "trickery, fraud and deceit." In May 1991, the U.S. Court of Appeals in Washington, D.C. reversed the findings, claiming that bankruptcy courts lacked jurisdiction over the matter.

Investigative reporter Danny Casolaro was investigating possible links between BCCI, Iran-Contra, and Inslaw. He called the covert operation, in which he believed the CIA was involved, "The Octopus."

The Justice Department started sharing the illegally obtained PROMIS software with other agencies, including intelligence agencies where PROMIS was modified for intelligence purposes and sold to foreign intelligence operations in Israel, Jordan, and other places. Michael Risconsciuto of the Wakenhut security firm has testified that he was contracted to install a "trap door" in the software to allow the CIA to tap into PROMIS software worldwide. It appears that the original petty crimes of the Justice Department have led to the exposure of a sensitive national security operation.

As Casolaro continued his investigation he started to receive death threats. He told his brother, "if there was an accident and he died, not to believe it." On August 11, 1991, Casolaro was found dead in the bathtub of a hotel room in Martinsburg, Virginia, where he had had a meeting with a U.S. Army Special Forces covert intelligence officer.

Following the death of Casolaro, Inslaw Attorney Elliot Richardson called for an investigation. "It's hard to come up with any reason for his death, other than he was deliberately murdered because he was so close to uncovering sinister elements of what he called "The Octopus," Richardson said.

After Judge Bason's ruling was reversed on technical jurisdictional grounds in 1991, the Senate started investigating the Inslaw scandal and found even more troubling information: its investigation was hampered by an unwillingness by Justice Department officials to cooperate, and because key documents were reported missing or lost by the Department.

According to sworn testimony before the Committee, high level Justice Department officials conspired to steal the PROMIS software and secretly convert it to use by domestic and foreign intelligence services.

Ronald LeGrand, Chief Investigator for the for the Senate Judiciary Committee told Hamilton and Richardson that a trusted Justice Department source had confided that Inslaw "was a lot dirtier for the Department of Justice than Watergate had been, both in its breath and depth."

After several Congressional investigations concluded wrongdoing by the Justice Department and called for the appointment of a special prosecutor, Attorney General William Barr in 1992 appointed lawyer Nicholas Bua to investigate the Inslaw scandal. Bua impaneled a grand jury, but dismissed it midway through the investigation, allegedly because it was giving credence to the allegations and constituted a "runaway" grand jury.

In June 1993 the Bua report was released. It cleared Justice officials of any wrongdoing in the case.

Inslaw Attorney Elliot Richardson issued a statement saying, "What I have seen of [the report] is remarkable both for its credulity in accepting at face value denials of complicity in wrongdoing against Inslaw and for its failure to pursue leads making those denials implausible."

On July 12, 1993 Inslaw submitted a 90-page rebuttal of the Bua report to Associate Attorney General Webster **Hubbell**. The rebuttal offered evidence that the Bua report was false. What Inslaw probably did not know at time, however, was that Webster Hubbell's and White House Deputy Counsel Vince Foster apparently were linked to both Iran-Contra and Inslaw through two Arkansas companies called Park-o-Meter and **Systematics**.

On July 20, 1993 Vince Foster was found dead in **Fort Marcy Park**. Three days later, attorney Paul Wilcher, allegedly investigating "The Octopus" was found dead.

After Inslaw owner Bill Hamilton distributed a report on the Inslaw scandal to each member of the House Judiciary Committee, Congressmen Jack Brooks (D-TX) and Charlie Rose (D-NC) tried to enact a bill that would force an investigation of the Justice Department and the death of Danny Casolaro, and pay reparations to the owners of Inslaw. Among the allegations in the bill:

The following criminal statutes may have been violated by certain high level Justice officials and private individuals:

18 U.S.C. Sec. 371—Conspiracy to commit an offense.

18 U.S.C. Sec. 654—Officer or employee of the United States converting the

property of another.

18 U.S.C. Sec. 1341—Fraud.

18 U.S.C. Sec. 1343—Wire fraud.

18 U.S.C. Sec. 1505—Obstruction of proceedings before departments, agencies and committees.

U.S.C. Sec. 1512—Tampering with a witness.

18 U.S.C. Sec. 1513—Retaliation against a witness.

18 U.S.C. Sec. 1621—Perjury.

18 U.S.C. Sec. 1951—Interference with commerce by threats or violence (RICO.)

18 U.S.C. Sec. 1961 et seq: Racketeer Influenced and Corrupt Organizations.

18 U.S.C. Sec. 2314—Transportation of stolen goods, securities, moneys.

18 U.S.C. Sec. 2315—Receiving stolen goods.

The bill, H.R. 4862 was introduced in the House on July 29, 1994, but died without any action by the Democratic leadership in the waning days of the 103rd Congress.

Under the new Republican leadership, Senator Orrin Hatch introduced a similar bill, S. 740. On May 3, 1995, the Senate voted to commit the bill, which would pay reparations to the owners of Inslaw, to the chief judge of the United States Court of Federal Claims for a report thereon.

According to John Crudelle of the New York Post, Webster **Hubbell** and Vincent Foster owned a small amount of stock in the Arkansas company **Systematics** that was also illegally selling the software. Both Hubbell and Foster provided legal representation for Systematics.

The ADFA/Coral/AIG Connection

The following account of clandestine banking operations involving an Arkansas agency created by Bill Clinton is even stranger than is intimated in the well documented story below. Time and space do not allow for additional facts mentioned in a 5 hour interview with Mark Swaney, who figures prominently in this article.

—From the staff of the **Ozark Gazette**

Activists seeking documentation that would support claims that the state of Arkansas was involved with money laundering on a massive scale may have found the missing link in their three year search.

Documents obtained by the Arkansas Committee show that the Arkansas Development and Finance Authority, a Bill Clinton signature project, was involved in a highly questionable, and possibly illegal, sixty-million dollar deal in which **ADFA** borrowed 5 million dollars from a Japanese bank in order to buy stock in a Barbados insurance company. The stock was not registered with the Securities and Exchange Commission.

The state of Arkansas was the lead investor in a deal which poured sixty million dollars through a Barbados company, **Coral** Reinsurance, which is currently under investigation by insurance regulators in New York, Pennsylvania, and Delaware as well as by Manhattan District Attorney Robert Morgenthau, lead prosecutor in the BCCI scandal. Additionally, the Ozark Gazette has recently been told that as a result of the release of the Coral documents the independent counsel, Kenneth Starr, is also investigating the deal.

Persons involved in the deal, which began in 1987 and ended in 1991, include Bob **Nash**, then president of **ADFA** and now Personnel Director of the White House, Robert Rubin, then president of Goldman Sach's investment bank and now Secretary of the Treasury, and Maurice Greenburg, president of American International Group, and a candidate in 1995 to be Director of Central Intelligence.

The American International Group is a 100-billion dollar, multi-national insurance company which founded Coral Reinsurance Company in 1987. The fact that **AIG** founded **Coral** was hidden from insurance regulators for at least 3 years and was only recently proven by the reluctant release by **ADFA** of the original stock placement memorandum. Maurice **Greenburg** as president of **AIG** is a very well connected businessman and a player in international politics. He serves as the chairman of the US-China Business Council and lobbied hard (and successfully) for the Clinton administration to sever the link between China's human rights record and renewal of China's most-favored-nation trade status. Members of the board of directors of **AIG** include Martin Feldstein, Harvard University economics professor and former chairman of the President's Council of Economic Advisors and Carla Hills, former U.S. trade representative. AIG's international advisory board is headed by Henry A. **Kissinger**.

The original deal was pitched to **ADFA** by Goldman-Sachs, a New York based securities firm which played an important role in the transaction. Goldman-Sachs had pledged to sell the stock for Coral and in addition pledged to buy the stock if for any reason the other investors could not hold it and were forced to sell. Goldman's president at the time was Robert **Rubin**, later appointed by the Clinton administration to succeed Lloyd Bentsen as the Secretary of the Treasury.

The Search Begins

Founded in 1990 as a student organization at the University of Arkansas, the Arkansas Committee's major focus was on Arkansas' involvement with the mysterious activities at the Mena airport during the 1980's. The Committee spent two years unsuccessfully trying to convince the state government to investigate links between major drug smuggler Barry Seal (also a government informant), who worked out of the Mena, Arkansas airport, and the U. S. Intelligence community.

Recently, two very respected investigative journalists, Roger Morris and Sally **Denton**, have published the most authoritative and highly documented account to date of events at the Mena airport between 1982 and 1986. Based on over 2,000 documents including the previously unpublished personal papers of Barry Seal, their article "The Crimes of Mena" in the July issue of Penthouse Magazine reveals the government's protection and cover up of drug smuggling, gun running and money laundering.

Realizing that personal accounts were not sufficient to convince skeptics, in the summer of 1992 the Committee began what would become its most difficult journey - finding enough hard evidence to convince the media (the court of last resort, the government having rebuffed two years of pleas to do the job itself) to investigate and write about Mena. And so they began trying to locate the long buried paper trail, armed only with the Freedom of Information Act and determination.

But what sort of hard documentation could they reasonably hope to find? The Committee's sources had on more than one occasion indicated that up to ten million dollars a week in illegal cash was going through Arkansas at the height of the Mena operation. Therefore the most logical course seemed to be to the hoary old cliché: follow the money.

For two important reasons, the Committee decided to look into the Arkansas Development Finance Authority (**ADFA**).

187

First, some admittedly circumstantial evidence linked ADFA to the Mena operations. Secondly, as a state agency, ADFA was subject to Arkansas's Freedom of Information Act, and so documents could be extracted from what was hoped would be an important source of information. Throughout 1992, the Arkansas Committee contacted numerous sources in their search for evidence that ADFA may have been involved in money laundering operations. Several people assured them that ADFA was indeed involved, knowingly or otherwise, with laundering many millions of dollars.

ADFA sells bonds as a state bonding agency, and it was alleged that many of the bonds were bought with drug money. But this meant that even if the bonds were purchased with black money, ADFA would still be in the clear, since ADFA could claim that they had no knowledge of the sources of the money used to purchase their bonds. Additionally, ADFA does not sell it's own bonds directly to the public, but instead uses a middleman - a bond underwriter - the perfect deniable link. Committee member Mark Swaney suspected that it was possible that ADFA had become involved in money laundering directly, so he began searching for other ways in which black money may have been moved with ADFA's involvement. In August of 1992, Swaney received what he felt was his first real break, when a source told him to look for ADFA's involvement with an insurance company.

Committee Hits Pay Dirt

Life not being like the movies, it took two years before the Committee was able to find any such link. In 1994, Swaney and the Arkansas Committee (in thus far their last official act as a group) sued **ADFA** for their auditor's working papers, after the documents were not forthcoming. The lack of interest on the part of the main stream press had not changed and the only attendees at the press conference announcing the suit were one reporter, and a camera crew from a public access television station. In a recent Arkansas Supreme Court ruling that has extended the power of the state's freedom of information act, Swaney and the Arkansas Committee were handed a unanimous victory when the court overturned the original decision by Judge Kim Smith. The new ruling places the burden of obtaining public documents held by private companies on the relevant state agency. The decision means that state agencies cannot circumvent the freedom of information act by insuring that they are not in possession of sensitive documents. (Oh, we don't have "physical possession" of that document - because we gave it to our lawyer to keep...)

The Committee reasoned that the public audits of **ADFA** were unlikely to provide any useful information, however the working papers of the auditors should yield a much more complete and detailed picture of ADFA's dealings. Because the Committee members were not financial experts they decided to locate someone well versed in accounting and / or auditing to review the papers when and if they could obtain them. To this end, Swaney teamed up with well-known independent financial analyst and ADFA critic, Roy Drew.

In a conversation about their collaboration, Drew told Swaney that he had found evidence of **ADFA**'s involvement in a very strange deal with a certain Coral Reinsurance Company. Roy Drew had been reading the minutes of ADFA's board of directors meetings and found one paragraph (in thousands of pages) describing a deal where ADFA would borrow 5 million dollars from the Sanwa bank's Chicago branch to buy stock in Coral Reinsurance. Additionally, the minutes revealed that according to the terms of the loan ADFA did not have to repay the loan if it did not make as much money in dividends on the stock as it owed in interest on the loan. To the Committee, this seemed to be the long sought after link between ADFA and an insurance company, especially since there was no known connection to any other insurance business.

After finally obtaining an opportunity to examine the **ADFA** auditor's working papers, the Committee asked ADFA for copies of all documents relating to the Coral insurance deal. Derek Rose, PR man for ADFA, readily agreed to make the Coral documents available. On December 2, 1994 ADFA's auditors (Deloitte & Touche) allowed Swaney and Drew limited access to the working papers. On the same day Swaney visited ADFA and copied the entire Coral file that Rose had retrieved for him. While Swaney was copying the documents, Rose was apparently seeing the material for the first time. It quickly become obvious to Swaney that several documents contained in the file where very sensitive inter-office ADFA memos. One of the memos, apparently written in a panic by Bob **Nash**, indicated that he had been questioned about the Coral deal in 1992, and had been shaken by it. In addition, a letter written to ADFA by the Delaware Department of Insurance requested information concerning ADFA's involvement with Coral Reinsurance, and strongly suggested that they were investigating Coral Reinsurance.

Curiouser and Curiouser

After returning to Fayetteville, Swaney and the Committee began to study the documents in detail. Several facts were especially interesting given the background of the search. First, Coral Reinsurance was incorporated in the tiny Caribbean island of Barbados - a notorious haven for money launderers due to it's very lax banking regulations and tight corporate secrecy laws. If someone wanted to launder cash, this was a good place to do it. Second, the deal was structured in such a way as to prevent the reporting of the ownership of the stock to the IRS. Third, the stock certificate plainly stated that "these securities have not been registered under the securities and exchange commission act of 1933". The deal had all the earmarks of a clandestine arrangement designed to conceal the true ownership of Coral Reinsurance.

Further information gleaned from the documents showed that **ADFA**'s role in the deal was unique. There were several other investors, none of whom had any visible government connection. Also, ADFA's share of the stock was larger than any other investor, and ADFA had signed a "put agreement" with Goldman Sach's in which they obligated themselves to buy the stock of any other investor in the case that the investor found that they could no longer hold the stock, and Goldman could find no other qualified investor. Finally, in case ADFA couldn't hold the stock, Goldman Sach's would buy it. In no case was the Sanwa Bank ever to own the stock.

The total amount of stock in the deal was 1,000 shares at $60,000 per share for a total of 60 million dollars. **ADFA**'s portion was 84 shares for a total of $5.04 million. Another very interesting fact was that the money apparently never left the Sanwa Bank. The whole transaction was conducted on paper. Sanwa loaned the $60 million to the investors, who used it to buy the stock in Coral, which then redeposited the money back in the Sanwa bank in the form of a certificate of deposit. Also mentioned in the documents was the American International Group, a huge insurance company with international business and political connections. The documents indicated that Coral was going to re-insure **AIG** as part of its business.

Taken together, these facts indicated that this deal was indeed very strange. **ADFA** took no risk, since the loan with Sanwa guaranteed it a profit, and was secured solely by the stock.

ADFA did nothing more than sign papers, in exchange for a profit of $58,000. At first glance, any intelligent person would question a deal that promised something for nothing (indeed, it was later revealed that one of ADFA's legal advisors - John Selig of the Mitchell firm - did ask the crucial questions, "what's in it for AIG? why pay us for nothing?").

Swaney and Drew could not help wondering whether or not ADFA's role was to provide the appearance of legitimacy and liquidity so that the other investors would not be fearful of getting involved.

Roy Drew and Mark Swaney wanted to learn all that they could about the Coral deal before releasing the documents to the media, so that further information could be obtained before media involvement stirred up the situation. Roy Drew contacted the Delaware Department of Insurance to find out what their original interest in Coral had been and to see if they were still interested in obtaining the **ADFA** documents.

The Delaware Department of Insurance was in fact very interested in the documents and a series of strange phone conversations took place between Drew and his contact at the DDI.

Drew was told that **ADFA** had never responded to the DDI's request for information, so that they had no documenta-tion on the Coral-ADFA deal. Initially the DDI was very suspicious of Roy Drew, not being sure with whom they were dealing. They requested assurance from him that he was not a member of any official US government agency and that he was not working for ADFA or Coral.

Shortly after these initial exchanges Drew's original contact at the DDI was taken off the case and his superiors informed Drew that his contact had been instructed not to say anything more to anyone about case. Seeing no point in trying to get further information from Delaware about the case, Swaney and Drew decided to release the story to the media. A reporter for the business section of the New York Post, John Crudelle, had been following the progress of the Committee's efforts and in early January, 1995, Swaney mailed him the Coral documents.

Further Revelations

Things began to get even stranger on January 6, 1995. That day John Crudelle of the New York Post published a column which called attention to the whole deal involving Coral, **ADFA** and AIG. The story was only on the streets in New York for a few hours when Swaney received a call from a man who told Swaney he had been conducting his own investigation of Coral Insurance and **AIG** but had not realized until then that the connections led to people now in the White House. When Swaney asked him to identify himself, he declined to do so, for fear of retaliation.

We will call him Mr. Anonymous. It seems that Mr. Anonymous is an insurance man in New York City - a competitor of **AIG** - and at sometime in the last two years he became very suspicious of **AIG** because its affiliates were offering insurance at premiums way below market rates. Mr. Anonymous told Swaney that he could not believe that a legitimate insurance company could stay in business offering such low rates. Mr. Anonymous suspected that he was in competition with an illegal enterprise, and began poking around in the affairs of AIG. At some point after that, Mr. Anonymous became frightened, and dropped his investigation, because he believed that the repercussions were damaging his own business. Mr. Anonymous also told Swaney (and John Crudelle of the New York Post) that **AIG** and it's relationship with Coral Reinsurance was under investigation by the insurance regulators of Pennsylvania and New York.

Mr. Anonymous had discovered that **AIG** was doing a lot of business through the island nation of Bermuda. He then flew to Bermuda to examine the records of AIG's business dealings. In conversation with Swaney, Mr. Anonymous said that one of the companies that he believed to be underwriting policies issued by **AIG** had given a Fort Smith, Arkansas address. When Swaney asked for the name of the company, Mr. Anonymous told him it was Beverly Indemnity.

Intrigued by the new connections to Arkansas, Swaney requested, and received, copies of the documents that Mr. Anonymous had obtained in Bermuda. The documents for Beverly Indemnity of Bermuda contained the names of two of its officers, Robert Pommerville, and Ronald C. Kayne. Swaney suspected that Beverly Indemnity was controlled by the well-known Beverly Enterprises of Fort Smith, AR - a call to Beverly Enterprises revealed that Pommerville did indeed work for Beverly Enterprises. Pommerville was later identified as the General Counsel for Beverly Enterprises. At the time of the Coral Insurance deal, Beverly Enterprises was owned and controlled by Stephens, Inc.

In a telephone interview Mr. Pommerville stated that Beverly Enterprises has an ongoing relationship with one of AIG's affiliates. The National Union Fire and Home Insurance company of Pittsburgh, Pennsylvania insures the Beverly Enterprises nursing homes. In turn, Beverly Indemnity, Inc. reinsures National Union. Mr. Pommerville stated that the arrangement was a step toward Beverly Enterprises becoming self-insured. Beverly Enterprises has a current connection with **ADFA** though Bobby Stephens (no relation to Stephens Inc.) who is a member of the board of directors of both ADFA and Beverly Enterprises. The minutes of the board of directors meeting at which the board members voted to buy the Coral Reinsurance stock show that Bobby Stephens was absent.

Beverly Enterprises has an intriguing past association with **ADFA**. Those with long memories will recall that in the year after the Coral deal, a controversy erupted involving Beverly Enterprises, ADFA and former Arkansas Attorney General Steve Clark. At that time ADFA was considering a deal involving a bond issue which would have benefited Beverly Enterprises. Clark interrupted the public ADFA meeting involving the issuance of the bonds and claimed that the Stephens family, then the principal owners of Beverly Enterprises, had offered him a $100,000 campaign contribution (translated- bribe) if he would remain neutral on the deal involving ADFA and Beverly Enterprises. Other observers of state politics have claimed that **Clark**'s later problems originated with his grandstand announcement "in front of God and everybody" at the ADFA meeting.

Soon after the columns by John Crudelle appeared in the New York Post, other media began to be interested in the Coral Reinsurance deal. Business Insurance magazine reported on the Coral deal. An **AIG** spokesperson denied that **AIG** had organized Coral Reinsurance. Other industry sources told John Crudelle that $450 million dollars had suddenly appeared in Coral's account in just the last two weeks of 1987. Investigators have been unable to identify the source of the cash infusion.

Further columns on the story by John Crudelle indicated that **AIG** was attempting to distance itself from Coral and would only say that Coral wrote reinsurance policies for **AIG** - investigators for insurance regulators wanted to know if **AIG** actually in fact owned Coral. This is the reason that the Delaware Department of Insurance originally contacted **ADFA** in 1992. The DDI wanted to see the stock placement memoranda because such memoranda usually include information on who is starting the company, what the nature of the business is, and with whom it intends to do business.

In mid December Swaney had written another FOIA request to **ADFA**, asking for copies of documents relating to the Coral deal which were not in the original file obtained on the second of December. Two of documents requested were:

1) the confidential stock placement memoranda.

2) the written legal opinion promised by **ADFA** to Coral which was supposed to state that ADFA had legal authority to buy the stock in first place.

ADFA responded to the FOIA by stating that all of the Coral documents in ADFA's possession had already been copied by Swaney.

By the middle of February 1995 it was determined that **ADFA**'s response, while technically true, was simply a dodge since the requested documents were in fact in the possession of one of ADFA's attorneys, Ann Ritchie-Parker of the Mitchell Firm, a prestigious Little Rock law firm.

When the long sought after memorandum was finally obtained, it revealed that indeed, **AIG** had founded Coral Reinsurance.

While all of these facts were in themselves very interesting, an event in the latter part of February, 1995 added yet another twist to this bizarre story. In an article in the February 20 issue US News & World Report it was revealed that Maurice Greenburg was being promoted by Senator Arlen Specter as the successor to Woolsey as Director of Central Intelligence. Jack Wheeler, writing in the February 22 issue of Strategic Investment Newsletter, stated that the Clinton administration had sent up a "trial balloon" in January on the possibility of nominating Greenburg as the new Director of Central Intelligence. There was very little support for a Greenburg nomination. Did the newly published details of the Coral-**ADFA** deal deflate the balloon?

At about the same time Bob **Nash**, author of the "panic" memo, and former President of **ADFA** was made the director of White House personnel by Clinton. On February the fifth, Lloyd Bentsen, former Secretary of the Treasury, was appointed to the board of directors of AIG.

Bentsen's successor at the treasury was Robert Rubin, the President of Goldman Sachs at the time of the Coral/**ADFA** deal.

By the middle of February the stories written by Crudelle were attracting attention in the Arkansas press. Andrea Harter of the Democrat Gazette began a month long investigation into the Coral deal. The story appeared March 5, 1995 and revealed even more extensive connections between AIG/ **ADFA**. In the year preceding the purchase of Coral stock by ADFA, an **AIG** affiliate had managed over one billion dollars worth of ADFA's bonds. Having been founded in 1985 and starting business in 1986, by early 1987 ADFA had only been in business a little over a year. AIG's involvement with that much of their bonds so early in ADFA's history indicates a very strong relationship. Once again, considering that the Arkansas Committee had been told that US Intelligence had indeed laundered money through ADFA, and that the sale of ADFA's bonds was one such vehicle for doing so, Maurice Greenburg's connections to international politics and intelligence was very interesting.

As a result of Andrea Harter's investigation it was determined that the written legal opinion referred to in the Coral/ **ADFA** documents did not exist. Ms. Ann Parker-Ritchie claimed that "everyone agreed at the time that it was legal for ADFA to purchase the stock" so the opinion was never written down. Although this point was not challenged by Harter in the Democrat Gazette article, John Haman noted in the following week's edition of the Arkansas Times that Article 12, Section 7 of the Arkansas State Constitution flatly prohibits the state of Arkansas from owning any stock. Thus it would appear that ADFA's purchase of the Coral stock was illegal. Mark Swaney comments "no wonder they didn't write the opinion down on paper!"

Aside from the cloak-and-dagger aspects of the Coral Reinsurance deal, the Arkansas Committee's investigation of **ADFA** reveals some interesting points concerning this center of financial power in Arkansas. First is the fact that ADFA's dealings do not have to have anything to do with helping the economy of Arkansas directly. Aside from a small profit of $58,000 on a 5 million dollar loan, who in Arkansas benefited from the Coral deal? Who in Arkansas benefits from the billions of dollars in bonds which ADFA sells? Certainly the bond daddies of Stephens and other underwriters. Roy Drew has studied the dealings of ADFA and calls the agency "an unregulated savings and loan." ADFA has claimed that they have oversight in the form of independent auditors. In fact, the legislation that created ADFA in 1985 specifically prohibited ADFA from using the Joint Legislative Auditing Agency - the state's public auditors. Was this an attempt to circumvent the Freedom of Information Act? Documents obtained by the Arkansas Committee from Deloitte & Touche (ADFA's auditors) show at least one example of the auditors covering up for ADFA and was reported in the February 17, 1995 issue of the Arkansas Times.

Auditing firms are noted for being more than willing to please their customers, as in the infamous Silverado Savings and Loan case.

The auditor's papers also showed that the board of directors of **ADFA** on four occasions approved loans in spite of their own staff's recommendations that the companies not receive the loans. Two of the loans have since defaulted. In three of the four cases, the companies were owned by people who were friends of the members of the board of directors. In one of the four cases, $400,000 was loaned to the husband of a long time ADFA employee, and former secretary to Bob **Nash**.

Considering that the board is entirely appointed by the governor, the possibilities for political corruption are obvious. Consider that the flow of billions of dollars is controlled essentially by one man. Consider the unaccountable power which flows to the person who can decide which underwriters get to slop at the trough.

Regardless of the outcome of the five separate investigations into AIG-Coral and **ADFA**, the results of the investigations of the Arkansas Committee have revealed a source of unaccountable power which is inconsistent with a democratic government.

For Committee members (such as Mark Swaney, Charlie Reed, Carol Conger, and John Benedict) it means that they may at last receive attention for what they have been trying to point out, and not how it might affect anyone's political fortunes.

For those who may only get their information from daily newspapers, here is a brief background of what became known as the Mena Connection. In 1982, the near legendary drug smuggler, turned DEA informant, Barry Seal relocated his operations from Louisiana to the small town of Mena, Arkansas. Shortly thereafter, locals began to notice strange occurrences at the airport.

Over the next two years, local law enforcement officials heard stories of drug smuggling, gun running, illegal aircraft modifications, money laundering, and paramilitary training in the surrounding hills. Police began an investigation, only to have it taken over by the federal government. After two more years, through 1986, local and federal investigators had what they believed to be solid evidence of these crimes, only to see the United States Attorney refuse to present their evidence to the eventual grand jury.

Later, these investigators, and members of the grand jury themselves, complained loudly to the press that the case had been mishandled. When in October of 1986, Barry Seal's airplane was shot down over Nicaragua (the opening chapter of the infamous Iran/Contra affair) it became obvious to some observers that there had in fact been a cover-up of the alleged activities at the Mena airport.

Reasoning that even if the federal government had covered up what had occurred at Mena, it was still possible for the state government to investigate the situation, the Arkansas Committee's early strategy was to press for state investigation of Mena. From 1990 through early 1992, the Committee wrote letters, organized demonstrations, visited the offices of state officials, collected evidence and held press conferences, all in an attempt to pressure officials into reopening the case at the state level.

Failing to persuade officials to act, the Committee could not help but wonder why. Soon, they were faced with a previously unthinkable conclusion - it was as much an inside job as anything else.

Suspecting that Governor Bill Clinton had reason to hide such state involvement, the Committee decided to go public. Up to this point the Committee had been treated fairly and on occasion, even praised by the local media. However, now that the Committee was pointing an accusing finger at the local hero, the media began to turn against the people who were asking for simple justice.

At every step of the way, it has been an uphill battle. They have been accused of being dupes of the Republicans, of being cat's-paws of dark political forces. Mark Swaney, the leader of the group, has vivid memories of being angrily accosted by the editor of a liberal newspaper, zealously defending Bill Clinton against these infidels. The veracity of the accusations, that Clinton may have had knowledge of CIA involvement with Mena was not the point, the editor insisted. If we don t have Clinton, who do we have?

They found themselves in the uncomfortable position of being praised by right-wingers, who had their own agendas, and vilified by liberals, who feared that any serious criticism of the shining hope of the Democratic party might mean four more years of George Bush. In few instances was the truth ever the issue, but merely how the facts might affect the political fortunes of Arkansas' favorite son.

Information the group supplied became the basis for articles in The Nation, The Washington Times and Village Voice, as well as providing groundwork for exposes on television programs such as "A Current Affair," and 'Now It Can Be Told."

However, in May 1992, the efforts to tell the truth about

Mena slid off-track when Time magazine, attempting to discredit the allegations, printed a major story purporting to tell the truth about the events in Arkansas, especially regarding connections to Bill Clinton, who was beginning his rapid ascent to the White House. The direction of the story was that it was much ado about nothing.

Whitewater grand jury subpoenas ADFA records

*—This article by Andrea Harter appeared in the **Arkansas Democrat-Gazette** February 14, 1996*

The federal grand jury looking into the Whitewater Development Corp. has subpoenaed records from Arkansas' bond agency in a search for information on four companies that received money from state coffers.

The Feb. 9 subpoena orders the Arkansas Development Finance Authority to turn over copies of all files, including private correspondence, concerning POM Inc., Southern Development Bancorporation, Pine Bluff Warehouse Inc. and Can-AM Absorbents Inc.

POM Inc. was first named in a grand jury subpoena presented to Gov. Jim Guy **Tucker** on Jan. 13. It is a parking meter manufacturing company in Russellville that was owned by Seth **Ward**, father-in-law of former Associate Attorney General Webb **Hubbell**. **ADFA** loaned POM $2.75 million in the late 1980s. The loan was repaid in 1989.

The Southern Development Bancorporation, based in Arkadelphia, was founded in 1988. The corporation owns the Elk Horn Bank & Trust Co. in Arkadelphia, which had assets as of mid-1994 of $100.5 million. It was started as a joint venture of Little Rock-based Winthrop Rockefeller Foundation and Shorebank Corp. of Chicago. Levi Strauss Foundation contributed heavily to the fund.

Southern Development was promoted as a commercial bank interested in providing loans to small businesses. In May 1987 the company sold $4.2 million in common stock to investors. **Systematics** Inc. (now owned by Alltel Corp.), Arkansas Best Corp., Arkla Inc. and the Walton Foundation were among investors buying into the stock offering.

The stock was offered to **ADFA**, but the agency, on the advice of lawyers, declined to buy stock. SDC's subsidiary, Southern Ventures, had solicited ADFA in 1993 to buy stock in the company.

According to a letter written Sept. 21, 1993, by Bill Wilson, **ADFA** interim president, the agency said it would not invest in Southern Ventures because "it would be inappropriate to ignore legal risks presented" by restrictions on ADFA's owning stock.

Dan Parker, **ADFA**'s attorney, said Tuesday that the agency's bond counsel, John Tisdale with Wright **Lindsey** & Jennings, had advised the agency not to buy the stock.

Wilson's letter says: "**ADFA** is wary of setting precedents that would be extremely difficult to control and could have a severe long-term impact on the Authority's ability to remain self-supporting."

Wilson's letter contradicts a move made by **ADFA** in 1987, when the agency borrowed $5 million from Sanwa Bank of Chicago to invest in a Barbados company, Coral Reinsurance

Co. Limited, an offshore stock deal ADFA cashed out of after three years that netted ADFA about a $240,000 profit. The Mitchell firm, ADFA bond counsel at that time, had approved that stock purchase.

ADFA's relationship with the Pine Bluff Warehouse Co. could not immediately be determined Tuesday. The agency loaned the company money through the Industrial Development Bond Program in the early 1980s. ADFA said it is researching the transactions.

ADFA issued a $375,000 bond to Can-Am Absorbents Co. in Bryant for expansion projects in 1992. The company manufactures cat litter, oil and gas absorbents and abrasive bauxite.

In October 1995, the Senate Special Whitewater Committee subpoenaed **ADFA** documents related to Dan **Lasater**, a former Clinton campaign contributor and business associate. **Lasater** was a principal in two companies that underwrote millions of dollars in bond issues for 16 housing projects administered by ADFA.

All articles reprinted with permission

Epilogue

"There has not been a single, solitary soul to accuse me or my wife of doing anything illegal, not only in the White House, in the presidential campaign, or in the govenor's office"

—*President Bill Clinton, in an interview with the Los Angeles Times*

"Clinton defenders like to talk of a 'cover-up without a crime,' choosing to ignore that a cover-up **is** a crime when it involves lying to federal investigators and Congress, destruction or concealment of documents and interference with federal agencies investigating possible wrongdoing, all of which appear to have occurred.

These crimes have a name: obstruction of justice...The (C)onstitutional issues of Watergate and Iran/contra may not be present in this Administration's transgressions, but ethical and moral breaches are no less troubling"

—*Doug Ireland* **The Nation** *February 19, 1996*

Addendum:

On February 20, 1996 Robert Hill and Herby Branscum were indicted in federal court on 11 counts of fraud, misapplying bank funds and lying to the IRS and the FDIC. Specifically, the indictment charges that Branscum and Hill diverted $11,700 in bank funds to various political campaigns, including Bill Clinton's 1990 race for govenor of Arkansas, then tried to hide the transactions from federal regulators. After Clinton's successful 1990 gubernatorial campaign, he named Branscum to the five-member Arkansas Highway Commission.

(SEE: Robert Hill, Herby Branscum)

A little something about the author—

Brian Wilson, nationally known talk show host and TV personality who has had audiences in New York, Washington, DC, Atlanta, Baltimore and Houston talking, cursing, laughing and/or blushing for 30 years, has just released his latest work: **"the little black book on WHITEWATER"**, a compendium of all that has come to be known as "Whitewater". Wilson says,"It's the Who, What, Where and When--but not the Why. If I knew that part, this wouldn't sell for $12.95 (if you paid more, THANKS!)"

Wilson is a 30 year veteran of radio and television. Despite being a native of Wayne, New Jersey, Brian began his radio career in erotic Baton Rouge, Louisiana. While earning a BA degree in Psychology at Louisiana State University, he began doing his show door-to-door, simultaneously maintaining his dual Amway/Tupperware route, before moving up to posh broadcasting jobs in the prestigious "Morning Drive" positions in Houston, Atlanta, Baltimore, Washington, DC as well as two tours of duty in New York City.

While in New York, Brian made numerous guest TV appearances on major network shows such as "Good Morning America", "Entertainment Tonite", "ABC Evening News with Peter Jennings", CNN's "Take Two", and "Geraldo" as well as starring in the premier episode of ABC's "Anything For A Laugh", a weekly sit-com.

According to a New York Times article on New York radio, Brian is "...quite funny, outspoken and pulls no punches when it comes to having a good time with his audience. Despite his mild eccentricity of wearing the full dress uniform of a French Foreign Legionnaire and carrying a quart of sterno in his canteen, he functions quite well with his occasionally wistful charm and boyish good looks."

Brian wasn't born yesterday and resides in bucolic northern Maryland, well out of gun range of the streets of Baltimore. His four children are scattered about the country, draining their father's savings in their relentless, if not rhetorical, pursuit of higher learning.

For future reference, we should bear in mind Brian's inspiring words before the Senate Whitewater Committee. And no doubt we will.

TEAR OUT THIS PAGE

For Additional Copies of This Great Book....

Mail $12.95 (plus $2.00 S&H) Cash, Check, Money Order, Gold Coins or Negotiable Bonds to:

Myrmidon Press
P.O. Box 632
Monkton, MD 21111

Name: _____

Address: _____

_____

City: _____

State/Zip: _____

Visa/MC:_____Exp _____

Copies:_____(10% discount for 10 or more)